PRAISE FOR

The Lifestyle Business Owner

"Aaron Muller cuts right to the chase on what you need to do to own a profitable business that runs without you."

—MARCI SHIMOFF
#1 *New York Times* best-selling author
of *Happy for No Reason* and *Chicken
Soup for the Woman's Soul*

"This practical book is full of proven strategies and techniques you can use immediately to increase your sales and profitability—from the first day."

—BRIAN TRACY
author of *Now, Build a Great Business*

"A must-read for anyone who wants to be a business owner. If you've ever dreamed of owning a business in your community, making a six-figure income, and working as little as five hours a week, then you'll love this book."

—GINO WICKMAN
Creator of EOS and author of the award-
winning, best-selling book *Traction*
www.eosworldwide.com

"Aaron Muller opened my eyes to the world of buying and running a business (or two or more) as a way to express your values, have fun, be creative and make enough money to have everything you need...including time for life's non-material pleasures. He speaks clearly, believably and honestly, giving you a great foundation to consider whether lifestyle business ownership is for you."

—VICKI ROBIN
co-author of *Your Money or Your Life*

"*The Lifestyle Business Owner* is a must read for every entrepreneur and business owner. Aaron gives you a step-by-step approach to purchasing and owning a business that runs without you. Absolutely amazing!"

—DR. ERIC J. SCROGGINS
author of *Vision Blockers*

"A comprehensive guide for the budding to the seasoned entrepreneur. I enjoyed the straightforward step-by-step processes that Aaron Muller describes in what it takes to become a lifestyle business owner. Having been in business for over 20 years, I found many strategies in this book that I plan to implement in my own business. A great book on how to make your business work for you! A true joy to read!"

—DAVID LIATOS
founder of CPA *Seattle PS*

"A straightforward recipe for success! I wish I'd read it years ago."

—KEIL A. LARSEN
Attorney at *Reed Pruett Walters PLLC*
www.rpwlawfirm.com

"A revolutionary paradigm shift on what it means to own a small business."

—BOB BAGGA
president and CEO of *BizX*

The Lifestyle Business Owner

the Lifestyle Business Owner

How to Buy a Business, Grow Your Profits, and Make It Run without You

AARON MULLER

NEW YORK

LONDON • NASHVILLE • MELBOURNE • VANCOUVER

The Lifestyle Business Owner

How to Buy a Business, Grow Your Profits, and Make It Run Without You

Published in New York, New York, by Morgan James Publishing. Morgan James is a trademark of Morgan James, LLC. www.MorganJamesPublishing.com

The Morgan James Speakers Group can bring authors to your live event. For more information or to book an event visit The Morgan James Speakers Group at www.TheMorganJamesSpeakersGroup.com.

ISBN 9781683506492 paperback
ISBN 9781683506508 eBook
Library of Congress Control Number: 2017910061

Cover Design by:
Rachel Lopez
www.r2cdesign.com

Interior Design by:
Chris Treccani
www.3dogcreative.net

In an effort to support local communities, raise awareness and funds, Morgan James Publishing donates a percentage of all book sales for the life of each book to Habitat for Humanity Peninsula and Greater Williamsburg.

Get involved today! Visit
www.MorganJamesBuilds.com

Dedicated to fellow entrepreneurs and aspiring entrepreneurs. The world would be different without those who are willing to enact change. I am grateful to be part of this journey with you.

NOTE TO READERS

This publication contains the opinions and ideas of its author. It is intended to provide helpful and informative material on the subjects addressed. The strategies outlined in this book may not be suitable for every individual and every situation and are not guaranteed or warranted to produce any particular results.

This book is sold with the understanding that neither the author nor the publisher is engaged in rendering legal, financial, accounting, or other professional advice or services. The reader should consult a competent professional before adopting any of the suggestions in this book or drawing inferences from it.

No guarantee is made with respect to the accuracy or completeness of the information or references contained herein, and both the author and publisher specifically disclaim any responsibility for any liability, loss, or risk, personal or otherwise, that is incurred as a consequence, directly or indirectly, of the use and application of any of the contents of this book.

CONTENTS

It's Not Easy Being a Business Owner

If you have ever tried to run a small business, you know that it is not easy being a business owner. When I was growing up, I dreamed about becoming an entrepreneur. Perhaps you can relate to this. There is something special and romantic about owning your own business, being an entrepreneur, and mastering your destiny. Our society also puts entrepreneurs pretty high up on the scale of esteemed professions. Entrepreneurs are the leaders, innovators, and job creators. Politicians often talk about encouraging more people to become entrepreneurs and small-business owners.

As romantic as it sounds to own your own business, however, the reality is that most small-business owners struggle. As a business broker and business consultant, I've had the privilege of meeting and talking with thousands of small-business owners every year. I listen to their dreams as well as their fears. I ask them about what's working and what's not working for them. They tell me what they are angry about and what they are struggling with. Invariably, the struggles of small-business owners can be summarized into four areas.

The first area of struggle for many business owners is lack of profits. To put it bluntly, they don't make enough money. I have met many business owners who put in very long hours and work harder than just about everyone else I know. Unfortunately, their businesses are just not very profitable. They mustered the courage to start the business of their dreams, and they did everything they knew to make their dreams a reality. These are people with passion and courage, and they are people who are not afraid to work hard. Every time I meet business owners who are struggling with lack of profits, my heart goes out to them. Despite all they have put in, they are losing money, barely making ends meet, or making so little money that they could have done better financially by doing something else.

The second area of struggle for many small-business owners is the stress related to having employees. Perhaps the employees do the minimum amount of work necessary just to get a paycheck, and the owners feel like they have to do the job themselves if they want things done right. Perhaps the employees are unreliable or untrustworthy and the owners have to constantly micromanage their staff. Perhaps the workplace is full of drama and office politics. People tolerate each other just to get by, but the team is, by and large, dysfunctional. One of the most common complaints I hear from small-business owners is this: "Aaron, having employees is so stressful that I wish I didn't have to have any employees."

The third area of struggle I hear many business owners complain about is the lack of time. Their employees get to go home at 5:00 p.m., but business owners often work late into the night. Their employees can, for the most part, stop thinking about work after they go home, but business owners worry about their company even after they have left the office. It is not uncommon for me to meet business owners who work sixty, eighty, or more hours per week. They wish they could spend more time with their loved ones or have more time to themselves, but they are responsible for the success of the company and just can't seem to run the company properly without putting in such long hours.

The fourth area of struggle for many business owners is the lack of meaning or enjoyment. They say to me, "Aaron, owning this business used to be fun, but it's not anymore." Or they say, "I used to get a lot of enjoyment out of running this business, but I don't get the same sense of meaning and enjoyment out of it anymore." Whereas the first three struggles are more in your face and easier to notice, the struggle with the lack of meaning or enjoyment is a deeper disquiet that people experience when they take the time to reflect. Not making enough money (and possibly going out of business) is like death by fire, and not feeling alive in and invigorated by your business is like death by ice. Slowly and quietly, your spirit and fire within are snuffed out.

Perhaps the reason so many business owners struggle for one reason or another is because of the reality of the time we live in. The economy today is no longer what it used to be. Job security is a thing of the past, and many business owners will attest to the fact that it is getting harder and harder to stay in business. Since the Great Recession of 2008, the Federal Reserve Bank has increased the US base money supply by over three trillion dollars. Think of it as printing money, except that the speed of printing is not limited by the printing press—the Fed simply has to type more zeros into the computer.

Ask any business owner or investor, and he or she will tell you that the economy is wacky today. In the good old days, you put money in the bank and earned interest. Today, interest rates are so low that, once inflation is taken into account, you actually *lose* money by putting it in the bank. In the good old days, you could buy a bond (meaning you lent money to a corporation or government) and earn interest. As of the writing of this book, there are trillions of dollars in government bonds in Europe that have negative yields. In other words, you can lend your money to a European country's government and get charged for it. If you think that makes no sense, neither do I.

The economy is making less and less sense to most people. Corporate layoffs can happen in a flash, and one can no longer count on lifelong employment with a company or depend on company pensions for retirement. And due to demographic shifts, neither can one depend on the government for retirement. In 1940, there were 159 workers paying into Social Security for every one retiree collecting from it. In 2010, there were fewer than three workers paying into Social Security for every retiree collecting from it.

To compound the problem, the world is changing faster than ever, and the speed of change is accelerating. Ten years ago, hardly anyone had a Facebook account. Today, not having a social-media strategy may really hurt your business. Ten years ago, most people had never heard of smartphones. Today, there are more users of smartphones than there are desktop users. Ten years ago, most consumers didn't take into consideration how environmentally friendly a business was when making their purchase decisions. Today, more and more consumers want to do the right thing, and they choose to purchase from companies that exemplify environmental and social stewardship.

The reality is that the world today is drastically different from the world ten years ago, and the world ten years from now will be equally foreign, if not even more foreign, compared to the world today. Our world is facing a storm of challenges. Geopolitically, tensions amongst countries are rising, and terrorist groups such as ISIS are instilling fear around the world. Environmentally, we are putting a tremendous amount of pressure on the earth, which produces symptoms such as the aquifers drying up, species becoming extinct, oceans acidifying, polar ice caps melting, fertile soils being degraded, grasslands becoming deserts, and a host of other problems that will only get worse as the world population goes from 7.5 billion in 2017 to more than 9 billion by 2038. To put it another way, we are adding the entire population of Seattle to the world every three days for the next twenty years. Demographically, many industrialized nations such as the United States are entering into a period with a larger aging population and a much smaller younger population, which can cause a host of problems—from not enough people paying into Social Security to economic deflation as the much larger older generation downsizes, cuts their spending, and sells the stocks and bonds in their retirement accounts to fund their increasingly higher health-care costs. A stock market with more sellers than buyers does not look good demographically for stock prices going up over time. Economically, we live in a world that is saddled with slow growth and massive debt, a world so interconnected that a crisis halfway around the world can cause a chain reaction around the globe, and a world where 95 percent of everything that moves from point A to point B in our just-in-time economy depends on the ever-dwindling, nonrenewable resource of oil. As the trend forecaster Gerald Celente likes to say, "Current events form future trends." The events happening right now are pointing to a world of increasing uncertainty and instability.

The good old days are gone. Economic conditions can change in a flash. In order for you to survive and thrive in the years ahead, you need to become more flexible than ever. In this new world we live in, those who cling to outdated ideas will likely be hurt. In this rapidly changing world, we need a new way of thinking about business ownership. Perhaps it is time for you to develop multiple sources of income instead of having only one source. Rather than owning only one business and spending all of your time running it, you could learn how to own multiple businesses and acquire the skills to make your businesses run without you. Instead of staying in the same line of business for years because it's what you've always done, perhaps it is time to learn about buying and selling companies so you can change directions should the trends in your current industry become unfavorable. Instead of owning a business that contributes to the greater problems we face as a society, perhaps it is time for you to own a business that contributes to the solution.

I neither had wealthy parents nor got a formal business education. I grew up in a small town in Washington and never went to college. At fifteen years old, I was doing menial labor washing trucks. One thing I did have was a strong desire to succeed and to make something of myself. I saved every cent I could and volunteered for more and more job responsibilities. By the time I graduated from high school, I had managed to buy 50 percent of the company from my boss. My success with the truck-washing company made me feel invincible and arrogant, thinking I could do no wrong in business. I learned my lesson the hard way after a painful failure with a retail business I got into. It was around that time that I committed to learning everything I could about business. I found that just because I was good at *something* didn't mean I was good at *everything*. In the years that followed, I bought an auto-repair shop, became a business broker, and bought more businesses along the way. Today, I own eight businesses that run without me having to be there. I spend my time helping people buy and sell companies as a business broker and coaching business owners on how to take their businesses to the next level; that is what I enjoy.

It is possible for you to own a successful business—one that gives you the income you desire, the free time you crave, and the meaning that feeds your soul. You don't have to come from a privileged family; I didn't. You don't have to possess a college degree; I didn't. You don't have to own eight businesses. Just start with one. When I started, I had no clue what I was doing. Everything I learned came from the school of hard knocks—the street smarts, if you will.

This book will change the way you think about business ownership. It will show you step-by-step how to add more income, free time, and meaning into your life, whether you already own a business or are just starting out as an aspiring entrepreneur. The book is divided into four parts. Part I introduces you to a new kind of business owner, one I call the lifestyle business owner. This section answers these questions: what exactly is a lifestyle business owner, and is it right for you? If you decide to become a lifestyle business owner, the rest of the book will show you how. Part II will teach you how to buy a business, Part III will show you how to take your revenues and profits to the next level, and Part IV will reveal how to make your business run without you.

I am so glad our paths have crossed. If you have read this far, I know there is something within you that wants change for the better. The tools and knowledge you gain from this book will show you how to own a thriving business (or businesses) in an uncertain world. I am excited to be part of your journey, and I look forward to supporting you along the way.

In appreciation,
Aaron Muller

PART I

It's Time for a New Kind
of Business Owner

CHAPTER 1

Meet the Lifestyle Business Owner

What comes to mind when you hear the word *entrepreneur*? Do you think of a couple of nerdy-looking kids starting a business in their garage, raising money from venture capitalists, and making it big in Silicon Valley? Do you think of someone who has had a long corporate career and finally decides to venture out and start his or her own business? Or do you think of someone who runs an Internet business, does not have an office, and easily passes you on the street without you ever knowing that he or she is an entrepreneur?

For many, the image of an entrepreneur brings up people such as Bill Gates, Steve Jobs, or Mark Zuckerberg. You know the stereotype: someone who is young and tech-savvy drops out of college and makes bazillions of dollars before he or she is thirty. Although this is one way to become an entrepreneur, it is certainly not the most common way.

Entrepreneurs come in all shapes and sizes. There is an entirely different class of entrepreneurs that live in the world of small business. Their goal is not to raise money from venture capitalists, take the company public, or sell the company for bazillions of dollars. Instead, they own a small business in the community, make, let's say, $100,000 to $200,000 a year, and spend five to ten hours a week on the business, ensuring that the employees and customers are happy and that the business continues to run well.

These small-business entrepreneurs will probably never become billionaires, but how many of us need to become billionaires in order to feel successful? For many of us, an income of $100,000 to $200,000 a year is more than sufficient to support our families and live a respectable lifestyle, and a work schedule of five to ten hours a week provides for plenty of free time to pursue other interests.

As you may have guessed, the description in the preceding two paragraphs is what it is like to be a lifestyle business owner. The business is built around the lifestyle you want instead of the business being a machine that consumes your every waking moment. A secret that all lifestyle business owners come to understand is that it is important to know how much is enough. Let's suppose you own a small business that generates $100,000 per year in income for you and that only requires you to work five hours a week. Is this enough income and free time to support the lifestyle you want? If you feel like you need more income, how about owning two small businesses, each making you $100,000 per year and each requiring five hours a week of your time to monitor, so you now have $200,000 a year in income and a work schedule of ten hours a week? How about owning three small businesses, so you have an income of $300,000 a year and a work schedule of fifteen hours a week?

If what I have described sounds too good to be true, know that these lifestyle business owners are all around you—you just never hear about them in the media. The media loves sensational and glamorous stories such as college dropouts becoming billionaires before they are thirty. It is great to become a billionaire or a multimillionaire within a few years, but how likely is it that that will be you? Thousands and thousands of new start-up companies fail every year, and in the news you hear only about the one company that succeeds. It is great that the founders of this one company became billionaires, but the founders of the rest of those start-ups are still broke.

In contrast, the kinds of businesses that lifestyle business owners own are rarely sensational or glamorous. Take my auto shop as an example. I have owned an automotive-repair facility in the community for more than fifteen years; it gives me over $200,000 a year while requiring me to spend about five hours a week monitoring it. Although the lifestyle sounds attractive and perhaps even sensational, people usually do not disclose their income or work schedule to the media. All the media sees is an auto-repair shop that fixes cars in the community, and there is nothing exciting to report.

I am trying to open your eyes to the world of lifestyle business owners. Chances are you do not hear much about them in the media because most lifestyle business owners do not own businesses that are glamorous or media worthy. These people are just small-business owners in your community. They never grow their businesses to have revenues in the hundreds of millions of dollars; instead, they own one or several small businesses with revenues in the $1 million to $5 million range. Instead of having hundreds or even thousands of employees, a lifestyle business owner might have fifteen employees or less. It is not that lifestyle business owners cannot grow their businesses but that they *choose not* to grow them.

You see, a small business is a lot simpler and easier to operate than a large company with hundreds of employees. A simpler operation means fewer chances for mistakes, lower financial risks, and the best chances for the owner to work very few hours and enjoy a wonderful lifestyle. Working only five hours a week running a big business is hard. Bill Gates founded Microsoft in 1975, worked long hours for many years, and finally became an absentee owner of the business in 2006 to dedicate his time to the Bill and Melinda Gates Foundation. In other words, it took him thirty-one years to become an absentee owner of a big business. In contrast, small-business owners can usually become absentee owners in as little as one to four years, depending on the current state of their business.

Let me be clear here. Not everyone wants or needs to be an absentee business owner. A lifestyle business owner is someone who builds a business around his or her desired lifestyle. Some people enjoy working in their business but just don't want to work sixty hours a week. If working twenty hours a week is what you desire, you can build a lifestyle business that allows you to work only twenty hours a week. Rather than put profits and growth above all else, lifestyle business owners design businesses around their values and the lifestyle they desire.

Becoming a lifestyle business owner may seem complicated, but it actually takes only three steps. Step one: you've got to own a business. If you don't currently own a business, the first step is to own one. Now, most people think that to own a business, you've got to start one from scratch. That's the image of the entrepreneur popularized by the media—someone who starts a business from scratch, makes an innovation commercially successful, and becomes really wealthy in the process. The truth is that starting a business is only one way (and often the riskiest and most expensive way) to become a business owner. There is another way to become a business owner that most people don't think about, which is to buy an existing business. In the chapters that follow, I will show you why buying a business is often cheaper, less risky, and more profitable than starting one. I will also show you exactly how to do it, but more on that later.

Once you own a business, step two of becoming a lifestyle business owner is to increase profits. Without enough profits, you will not be able to pay for the lifestyle you want. Without enough profits, you will not be able to afford to hire the right people, who will allow you to work fewer hours. Unless you buy a business that is perfect in every way to begin with (which almost never happens, by the way, as every business you buy will need some tweaking), you will need to implement some tweaks so that you can take your company's profits to the next level.

Step three, the final step in becoming a lifestyle business owner, is to empower your employees so your business can mostly run without you. This is the point at which you switch your focus from growing the company's revenues and profits to designing your business around your lifestyle and values. Many business owners choose to hire a general manager so they can gradually step back and work fewer hours. Many business owners also implement initiatives that leave a legacy. It's one thing to own a profitable business, but it's something else to own a business that really contributes to society. What's the impact of your business on the environment? What's the impact of your business on the local community? What's the impact of your business on the well-being and happiness of your employees? Business owners who succeed at the third step do things not because they have to but because they care.

If becoming a lifestyle business owner sounds exciting to you, the good news is that a number of developments have taken place in the last ten years that make it easier than ever to become one. It used to be difficult to find a business for sale.

But there are now websites that lists thousands and thousands of small businesses for sale. More business owners are starting to see selling their businesses as a way of transitioning into the next phase of their lives. In fact, more business owners are planning ahead and seeing the sale of their businesses as a part of their exit strategy. Business brokering is no longer an obscure profession. People seek out business brokers to help them buy a business, just as people seek out real-estate brokers to help them buy a house.

It is not only easier than ever to buy a business but also the right time for building a lifestyle business. More tools than ever have been developed to help businesses become more profitable. More business owners are coming to the realization that money and growth are not everything and that having quality of life, free time, happiness, and an enviable legacy are equally important goals to pursue. The days of building businesses that are cold, heartless cash machines are over. More and more consumers are choosing to spend money at businesses that have a heart.

We live in exciting times. It is estimated by BizEquity that 7.7 million US businesses will change hands over the next ten years. There will thus be 7.7 million chances to buy a business, grow it to the next level, and turn it into a lifestyle business. Unfortunately, many people will not succeed. As a business broker, I have seen people who choose not to heed my advice and end up buying a lemon. I have seen people who buy a great business and run it into the ground a few years later. I have also seen business owners who are considered highly successful by everyone around them, but in their hearts, they feel like a slave to their businesses.

The time has come for a learnable, step-by-step formula that shows people exactly how to buy a business successfully, how to run it well, and how to design it around their desired lifestyle and values. I will give you such a formula in this book. In learning this formula, you will also learn the following truths.

- In the fast-changing world we live in today, the people who win are those who know when to buy a business and when to sell it. The ones who lose are those who cannot be flexible and who cling to the outdated notion that one must own the same business for life.

- The people who win are those who know how to buy a good business. The ones who lose are those who think they must start a business from scratch.
- The people who win are those with the knowledge and skills to take their company profits to the next level. The ones who lose are those who let their profits be at the mercy of the economy.
- The people who win are those with the ability to make their businesses run without them. The ones who lose are those who do what they've always done and become slaves to their businesses.
- The people who win are those who build businesses with heart. The ones who lose are those who see their businesses as nothing more than heartless cash machines.

Much of what I have learned comes from my experience owning more than twenty companies (of which I still own eight today) as well as observing the operations of thousands of companies as a business broker over the last fifteen years. As a business broker, I get to meet with hundreds of business owners every year in every industry imaginable, study their business operations, and give them a valuation of how much their business is worth. I've met business owners who work five hours a week, and I've met business owners who work one hundred hours a week. I've seen businesses that were insanely lucrative as well as ones with owners who were struggling to get by. I've encountered business owners who were full of vitality and purpose and business owners who looked worn-out and exhausted. After running my own companies and studying the operations of thousands of other companies as a business broker, I have found consistent lessons in what works and what doesn't work in real life. It is my hope that I can share these lessons with you.

~ INVITATION TO ACT ~
What is your biggest takeaway from this chapter?

_____

_____

_____

_____

_____

_____

~ Free Training Videos ~
Visit www.LifestyleBusinessOwner.com
to download
your free training videos on
becoming a lifestyle business owner!

CHAPTER 2

The School of Hard Knocks

Things have not come easy for me in my life. My parents got divorced when I was five years old. My mom was the office manager at a company that sold paper sorters for copy machines. As a single mom, she worked hard to put food on the table. She couldn't afford to buy any snacks for my siblings and me. I remember that a treat for us was putting some butter and salt on a tortilla shell and baking it.

When I was in fifth grade, my mom remarried, and we moved to the San Juan Islands in Washington State. My stepdad was quite entrepreneurial and encouraged me to be the same. At eleven years old, I started my first business. I would go to the docks at 7:00 a.m., catch shrimp, bring them home, boil them, and bag them up—fifty shrimp to a bag. Then I would go back to the docks, where there were hundreds of boats and tourists, and sell each bag of fifty shrimp for $2.50. Since we lived ten miles out of town, I had to travel a long way just to cook the shrimp at home. As the summer progressed, I wanted to increase my production and asked my mom how I could cook the shrimp at the docks instead. My mom recommended a Crock-Pot. Looking back, I'm not sure why she didn't recommend a camping stove instead, because I suspect I was selling three-quarters-cooked shrimp from the Crock-Pot for the rest of the summer. My deepest apologies to any of you I might have made sick that summer.

The next year, my stepdad invested in me, and we got a fleet of bumper boats. I would sit at the docks and rent out the bumper boats. I had some medical issues at the time and couldn't be there to run the business. Thus, at the age of twelve, I hired my first employee to run the business for the month of August. I enjoyed being entrepreneurial with my stepdad's encouragement, but the romantic life of living on the island came to a crashing end when my mom and stepdad got divorced the next year. We moved off the island, and my entrepreneurial adventures felt like a thing of the past.

At age fifteen, I got my first actual job doing menial labor—washing trucks. I didn't do well in school, but I loved earning money. I would wake up at 5:00 a.m., wash trucks all day, and not be done until late into the night. While other kids were partying on the weekends, I was spending my weekends washing trucks with hot water and acid, which burned my skin.

Even though I was a laborer, my heart was set on becoming a business owner. I saved every cent I could from my job. I volunteered for extra responsibilities. By the time I was sixteen, my boss was impressed enough with me that he let me run the crew of truck washers. I managed the crew for three years and did such a good job that my boss didn't have to personally wash any trucks during that time. When I was seventeen, I told him that I very much appreciated the opportunities he had given me, but I wanted to be a business owner. I told him that I planned to start my own landscaping business. Not wanting me to leave, my boss offered to sell me 50 percent of his company.

I decided to take my boss up on his offer and became a co-owner of the truck-washing company. I was eighteen years old at the time, and many of my peers were heading to college. I looked at my life, asked myself whether college was right for me, and decided it wasn't. I was going to build the truck-washing company up to the next level. Through a combination of hard work, salesmanship, and luck, I brought in a lot of new business to the company and made over $100,000 a year before I was twenty years old. Well, my ego shot through the roof, and I thought I was a business genius. If I could do so well with the truck-washing company, there was no reason in my mind that I wouldn't also do well in another business.

So my partner (formerly my boss) at the truck-washing company and I started a retail business. That business turned out to be my four-year education at the school of hard knocks. The business lost a lot of money and got us into a lot of debt, and we struggled for four years with no end in sight. But neither my partner nor I wanted to give up. If we gave up on the retail business, it would mean we had failed. Neither of us wanted to admit defeat. If we just stuck it out and turned things around, we would have another success story in our lives instead of a failure story. I said to my partner, "What do you think about selling the truck-washing company so we can infuse money into the struggling retail business? It will give us a chance to turn the retail business around." The truck-washing business remained quite successful. My partner thought this was a good idea, but neither of us knew how to sell a business.

That very weekend, a solicitor put an envelope under my door. When I opened the envelope, I could not believe what it said. The letter inside was from a business broker asking if I had considered selling my business, and if so, to give him a call. I called him up. I didn't know what a business broker was, so he explained it to me. "Aaron, a business broker is very much like a real-estate agent. Instead of selling houses, though, we sell businesses and get paid a commission if the business sells. We try to get listings, and we try to find buyers who want to buy those listings. In other words, we match business sellers and business buyers together."

I liked his sales pitch and decided to list the truck-washing company for sale with him. Looking back, I realize that I didn't pick the most experienced broker. He had just gotten started as a business broker and had never sold a business before. He tried for six months to sell our truck-washing company but couldn't do it. During that time, he also didn't sell any of the other listings he had. Still, I saw something in the broker. At the end of six months, I said to him, "I am not upset that our listing agreement has expired and the company is still not sold. But just thinking about who would be a good fit to buy this business, I think you'd be perfect for it!"

He looked at me and said, "You are right, Aaron. I've actually fallen in love with your truck-washing company just listening to you talk about it for the last six months. I'll be making an offer next week."

The business broker ended up buying the truck-washing company from us. Throughout that period, our retail business continued to get worse. By the time the truck-washing company was finally sold, both my partner and I had doubts about whether it was the right thing to do to continue with the retail business. My partner said to me, "Aaron, if you don't want to continue with the retail business, I understand. Personally, I also need to decide if I want to continue with it or not." After a lot of quiet reflection, I decided to admit defeat. I paid off my debts from the retail business using my proceeds from the sale of the truck-washing company and walked away with nothing. My partner decided to stick with the retail business, ran it for seven more years, and ended up filing for bankruptcy. Looking back, I can see that the failure taught me to be humble. Sometimes the right thing to do was to admit I had failed and walk away from a bad situation.

By this time, it was the late 1990s. Everyone was buying dot-com stocks, including me. Out of sheer luck, I sold my dot-com stocks before the market crashed. I wish I could claim credit for the great timing, but I can't. I didn't know what I was doing with the stock market; I simply lucked out. The business broker who had bought our truck-washing company heard my story of the dot-com stocks and approached me with an opportunity. He said, "Aaron, I listed an auto-repair shop for sale. Would you have any interest in looking at it?"

"An auto-repair shop?" I exclaimed. "But I am not a mechanic! I might have played around with cars in high school, but let's just say, you don't want me fixing your car."

The business broker replied, "That's okay. The seller is not a mechanic either. He's never fixed a car in the sixteen years he has owned the business." That intrigued me. As I came to learn later, there are lots of businesses you can be successful at without having the technical know-how as long as you are good with management and have business-building skills. A person can be very successful as the owner of a plumbing business without knowing how to fix a toilet or a garbage disposal—that's what the plumbers you hire are for. In my case, being a mechanic would have helped me fix a car, but it would not necessarily have helped me be a business owner.

I ended up buying the auto-repair shop, doubling the business in a little over a year, and doubling it again over the next few years. I still don't know how to fix cars, but I fell in love with the idea of helping aspiring entrepreneurs succeed. I systemized the auto-repair shop so I had to spend only five hours a week monitoring it and became a business broker myself so I could help other people become successful business owners. In a few short years, I went from having almost nothing to my name to making a respectable living. Well, actually, you could say that I was living large. I got married, and we had our honeymoon in Italy. We built a custom house in the woods, which was supposed to be our dream home. I drove my five-hundred-horsepower Mercedes, and my wife had her BMW. In the eyes of society, we were a highly successful couple.

If you'd looked a little under the surface, however, you would have seen a different picture. Building our dream home stressed me to the max. My general contractor stole $200,000 from me. When the house was done, I didn't even enjoy it anymore. I drove fancy cars, but the car payment of two thousand dollars a month on my Mercedes alone was stressful. I worked a lot and didn't get to spend as much time with my kids as I wanted to. When the Great Recession of 2008 hit, everything came crashing down. I lost the house to foreclosure and went through a divorce. The fancy cars were gone, and I went from driving a brand-new Mercedes and Range Rover to driving a secondhand Chevy. I moved into the basement of my buddy's house and took a hard look at my priorities.

I began to ask myself a lot of hard questions. What really makes me happy? Is it being a business owner? Is it making lots of money? Why is it that I wasn't much happier after becoming a business owner and making lots of money? What stresses me out? How much do I really want to work? Ideally, what do I want to spend my time doing? If living large didn't make me happy, what kind of lifestyle would? I took an honest look at what had gone right in my life and what had gone wrong. After a lot of quiet reflection, I came to the realization that the key is not to always want more but to design my businesses around the lifestyle I want to live. Money and business are only means to an end, not an end in and of themselves. Ultimately, happiness should be my primary goal. I thought having more money would make me happy. When I was poor, that was certainly the case. But after a certain point, when I was living comfortably, making more money didn't necessarily increase my happiness. In fact, I often became stressed out with the increased work hours, responsibilities, and obligations.

With happiness as my main goal, I began to design everything I did around what would make me happy. I am not talking about surface pleasures, such as going to Vegas and having a good time. As much as I enjoyed the short-term pleasure of spending money, I wanted to live a life that mattered. I wanted to live a deeply happy, content, and fulfilled life.

So I asked myself, What does that look like? What are the main things I need to do to ensure that I live a deeply happy, content, and fulfilled life?

Today I am a different person than I was before. I used to think that the person with the most money wins. Today I think the person who is the happiest wins. I used to think that having more money, more growth, and more businesses was always better. Today I think that just having enough is better. I used to think that I needed to be rich before I could make a difference. Today I think I can make a difference in the world from exactly where I am right now—whether I am rich or poor. I don't put off making a difference until I am rich someday. I don't put off being happy until I am rich someday. I don't put off spending time doing what matters to me until I am rich someday. As Muhammad Ali once said, "Live every day like it's your last, because someday you're going to be right."

With this new mind-set, I made a number of adjustments in my life. At one point, I owned four auto-repair shops and was in conversation with a gentleman to buy a chain of eight more shops. I began selling off some of the shops I owned to bring my stress down to a more tolerable level. I owned a secondhand appliance store and decided to sell it as well, even though it was a profitable business. I realized that being in business with the right people was important to my happiness, so I got out of some partnerships that were not conducive to my happiness and formed new partnerships that were. Because I had decided to put my happiness first, I gave up a mobile-home park I owned and took some losses from another commercial property.

Today I am a much happier person than I was before. Currently, I own an eco-friendly truck-washing company, a green pressure-washing company, a search-engine optimization company, two auto-repair shops, an auto-glass franchise, a business brokerage, a matchmaking service, and even an online business selling eco-friendly pet-hair-removal rollers. I am always getting into new business ventures because I enjoy business, but everything I do is prefaced by the lifestyle I want to live. I love working with business buyers and sellers, so I spend a good amount of time working in my business brokerage company. I couldn't care less, however, about being a pressure washer, so I systemized that business, made the operations as eco-friendly as I could, and made sure the company could run without my daily presence. Having multiple sources of income allows me to be more resilient. Should one source of income fail, I still have others. I am always staying flexible as well. Should the industry trends become unfavorable to one of the businesses I own, I would consider selling it and maybe getting into something else. In case you are wondering, I am also remarried to the love of my life, and I feel grateful for my marriage and our five kids.

Over the last twenty-five years, I have learned the hard way what is truly important in life. Simply owning a business did not make me happy, but owning a lifestyle business has made a tremendous difference to the quality of my life. You know you own a lifestyle business when the business no longer runs you. You know you own a lifestyle business when your happiness is your number one priority. You know you own a lifestyle business when you are living comfortably, no longer feeling overworked, and feeling a sense of meaning with and contribution to the way your business is run. In the next chapter, I will give you the Lifestyle Business Owner Formula.

~ INVITATION TO ACT ~

What is your biggest takeaway from this chapter?

~ Free Training Videos ~
Visit www.LifestyleBusinessOwner.com
to download
your free training videos on
becoming a lifestyle business owner!

CHAPTER 3

The Lifestyle Business Owner Formula

There are three skills you need to master if you want to become a lifestyle business owner: how to buy a good business, how to increase its profits, and how to empower your people. I call this the Lifestyle Business Owner Formula, which is illustrated here:

Lifestyle Business Owner Formula

3 Empower your people

2 Increase profits

1 Buy a good business

The first step in becoming a lifestyle business owner is to buy a good business. I am not saying you cannot become a lifestyle business owner if you start your own business. But starting a business from scratch has many disadvantages, which you will discover in the next chapter. If you want to jumpstart your profits as well as your chances of successfully becoming a lifestyle business owner, buying a good business in the right industry is half the battle. I've met business owners who spend decades working tirelessly in their business, hoping that it will eventually become profitable enough so they can hire a manager and work fewer hours. While we'd all like to think that our success or failure is a direct result of our own efforts, sometimes our success (or lack thereof) has more to do with the greater industry trends and being in the right line of business in the first place. I will show you how to identify the right line of business to get into, how to tell what kind of business you can afford, and how to buy a good business from start to finish.

The second step in our formula is to increase the profits of your business. As I've said before, no business you buy will ever be 100 percent perfect, and chances are you will need to build up the company's revenues and profits to the next level. Even if the business is already profitable, I do not recommend stepping back and working fewer hours right away. The reason is that you don't know the business well enough yet. After you've bought a business, there will be plenty for you to learn. You'll need to know your employees. You'll need to know exactly how everything operates. You'll need to learn how to recognize the signs that things are working well and the signs that things are not working well. Only when you know your business inside and out can you confidently step back and monitor it from a distance.

The third and final step in the Lifestyle Business Owner Formula is to empower your people so that the business can, for the most part, run without you. This is where you design the business around your values and desired lifestyle. The first two steps in the formula are setting you up to be successful in the final step. I will talk here about the fears and concerns business owners have when it comes to leaving their employees in charge and not being there all the time. I will invite you to reflect on which goals are worth pursuing for you and which ones are not. I will show you how to become a background leader so that you can lead your business from afar, and I will discuss how your business fits into the greater fabric of society so you can implement programs that will enhance the contribution and well-being of your business and its stakeholders.

When I teach people how to become lifestyle business owners, they sometimes tell me, "Aaron, I know you can become a lifestyle business owner, but I can't." When I ask them why not, I often hear the same kinds of responses. These are valid concerns that hold people back, and I'd like to address them before we go any further.

Concern 1: Owning a business is too risky. People say, "Aaron, I can't do this because owning a business is too risky." Well, I agree. It is definitely a high-risk activity if you start a business from scratch. The media is full of stories and statistics about how 90 percent or more of start-up businesses fail within a few years. But starting your own business is not what I am proposing here. I want you to buy an existing business that is already profitable. In other words, you are turning a profit from day one.

When you buy a business, your risks are lowered dramatically. You already have a steady stream of customers. The business model has already been proven to work. If the seller of the business has consistently made $150,000 a year for the last fifteen years, it will be hard for you to lose your shirt unless you completely screw everything up. If you want to be a business owner but are worried about the risks, buying an existing business may be the path for you.

Concern 2: I don't have any money to buy a business. Here's the next objection I often hear: "But, Aaron, I don't have any money! How am I supposed to buy a business if I don't have any money?" Remember, I didn't have any money when I started either. I was fifteen years old when I started working at a truck-washing company, and I bought 50 percent of that company when I was eighteen. It took a lot of hard work, a lot of volunteering for additional job responsibilities without asking for increased pay, a lot of relationship building with my boss, a lot of saving every cent I made, and a lot of courage. I was willing to ask, to be rejected, and to negotiate, and I was also willing to accept buying 50 percent of someone else's company (instead of 100 percent) as a good first step.

If you don't have any money, start small or work hard to save some. You don't have to buy a million-dollar company as a first step. To excel in the fast-changing world we live in today, I always recommend that people have multiple sources of income, stay flexible, and not be married to the same business or income source for life. This means you can start small, buy a business you can afford, work your way up to having more money, and buy a larger business later on. At that time, you may decide to sell the first business you bought, or you may decide to keep it and continue running it as a lifestyle business owner.

Other solutions to the "I don't have money" objection include partnering with someone who has the money, borrowing from family and friends, and getting seller financing. I've done all three. Be careful when you partner with someone who has the money, however, because you want to make sure both parties have realistic expectations. Is one person going to put in all the money while the other person runs the business? What if the investing partner doesn't like the way the business is run? What if the business is short on cash in the future and the investing partner doesn't want to put in more cash? There are a lot of potential scenarios to discuss, but if you can work through the issues, an investing partner can provide you with the cash you need to buy a business.

Borrowing from family and friends is awkward for a lot of people, but I've done it, too, when my credit score was low because the custom house I built went into foreclosure. I didn't let having bad credit or a lack of money stop me from building my life back up. Fortunately, I have managed to pay everyone back.

Last but not least, you can borrow money from the seller of the business you wish to buy. Sometimes the seller is motivated enough to sell that he or she will lend you money to buy the business. This is called seller financing. Now, you may ask, "If the seller is so motivated to sell, doesn't that mean something is wrong with the business and I shouldn't buy it?" Not necessarily. Having a motivated seller may or may not mean something is wrong with the business. Sometimes the seller wants to move out of state. Sometimes the seller has an aging parent and wishes to spend more time with family. There may be a variety of reasons a seller would offer seller financing, including being required by the bank. In today's lending environment, if you are getting a loan to buy a business, many banks will also want to see the seller finance a portion of the purchase price.

When people say they don't have any money, it often means they are not willing to get the money. I've seen people who use money from their 401(k) accounts to buy a business, people who sell other assets they have and use the money to buy a business, and people who work really hard for many months or even years in order to come up with the money they need to buy a business. Don't let not having the money right now stop you. If you want something badly enough, you will find a way.

Concern 3: I don't have any business education or experience. If you don't know anything about running a business, it's okay. I didn't know anything about business when I started, either. I never went to college, never took a business class in high school, and learned everything the hard way. The important thing is your willingness to learn. Just by reading this book, you have a tremendous advantage over where I was when I first started, because I have compiled everything I've learned into an easy-to-follow, step-by-step format.

When you buy a business, the seller will also train you on the ins and outs of the business. Later in this book, I will share with you how you can stipulate in your offer the training you wish to receive from the seller. In addition to such training, there are lots of great resources that can help you become a lifestyle business owner if you are willing to learn. My company, for instance, offers online courses, seminars, and coaching programs specifically designed to help people become lifestyle business owners. There is a saying that when the student is ready, the teacher will appear. As long as you are willing to learn, the resources are there to help you succeed.

Concern 4: What you do is too hard. People say, "Aaron, what you are proposing is just too hard." I am not trying to downplay the hard work involved. Running a successful business is hard. Becoming a lifestyle business owner will take a lot of hard work. You will probably need to face your fears, do things that are hard for you, and make sacrifices along the way in order to achieve your goals.

If you are thinking to yourself that becoming a lifestyle business owner is too hard, may I suggest reminding yourself why you want to do this? Are you looking for more freedom in your life? Are you looking to feel more financially secure? Are you looking to spend more time with those you love? If you don't have a good enough reason why, you will be stopped by the obstacles along the way. Yes, becoming a lifestyle business owner will challenge you. But is it worth it? Only you can answer that question.

Concern 5: I don't have the time to do this. I also hear people say, "Aaron, that sounds great. But you don't understand. With the long hours I currently work, my family and social obligations, my need for rest and sleep…I just don't have the time to do what you suggest." Not having enough time is a common concern, and I've been there. It's hard when you feel like you are already stretched to the max and there is simply no way you can fit anything else into your life.

Fortunately and unfortunately, we all have twenty-four hours in a day. When I was fifteen, I was juggling going to school full-time, working full-time, and volunteering for additional responsibilities, hoping to learn the skills I needed to one day run the crew and convince my boss to sell part of his company to me. When the Great Recession happened, I was juggling going through a divorce, losing my house to foreclosure, running multiple companies, dealing with partner disputes, feeling responsible for meeting the payroll of my employees, and spending time with my kids. These were difficult periods of my life, but I knew I needed to make certain sacrifices in order to build a better future.

I don't know your current situation, and I know how hard it is not to have enough time. But let's be real here. We all have enough time if the desire is there. I can't tell you what changes you need to make in your life, but I can tell you that you are the only person who can figure it out. What kind of future do you want to build? And what sacrifices can you make today?

Concern 6: Not everyone can be a business owner. If you think that not everyone can be a business owner, I agree with you. Being a business owner or entrepreneur is not right for everyone. Some people are happier being the business owner, and some people are happier working for others. What makes you happy? I used to think that the person who makes the most money wins. And it is true that if you are a successful business owner, you can make a lot of money. But I've learned the hard way that happiness is more important. Being happy means doing what is right for you, and for many people, what's right for them is not owning a business.

I want you to do what's right for you. No one is forcing you to be a business owner. Do it only if you think it will make you happy. Start by asking yourself how you would like to spend your time and what makes you happy. If becoming a lifestyle business owner is part of the answer, then by all means trust yourself, and do everything you can to keep your fears in check.

Concern 7: I am too young, or I am too old. Yes, age can play a role in how people perceive you in business. If you are too young or too old, some people may not take you seriously. But don't let that stop you from achieving what you want. You may have to work a lot harder, but it is how we handle things that are hard for us that determines whether we ultimately succeed or not. I was eighteen when I bought my first business. As a business broker, I see people of all ages buying businesses. I know age can be a disadvantage sometimes, but you can't control your age. What you can control is how aware you are of your own influence on how people treat you. You may think that people will treat you the way they do no matter what you do. But the more attention you pay to your own influence, the more you will discover that you have more influence than you think.

Now that we have talked about the common obstacles that hold people back, I am dedicating the rest of this book to teaching you the Lifestyle Business Owner Formula. I will show you how to buy a good business, how to increase its profits, and, finally, how to make it run without you.

~ INVITATION TO ACT ~

What is your biggest takeaway from this chapter?

_____

_____

_____

_____

_____

_____

~ Free Training Videos ~

Visit www.LifestyleBusinessOwner.com

to download

your free training videos on

becoming a lifestyle business owner!

PART II

How to Buy a Good Business

Lifestyle Business Owner Formula

3 Empower your people

2 Increase profits

1 Buy a good business

CHAPTER 4

Why Buying a Business Is Often Smarter than Starting One

S teve and Abigail had always dreamed of owning their own restaurant. Steve had a stable job in corporate America, and Abigail was a stay-at-home mom. They had a ten-year-old daughter and a seven-year-old son. Whenever Steve and Abigail weren't busy working or taking care of the kids, they daydreamed about turning their passion into a business. Cooking was the one passion that really bonded them together. On a cold winter's day, Steve loved to make linguine with shrimp, clams, mussels, and mushrooms in a wine, butter, and garlic sauce and pair it with a delightful salad consisting of organic greens, gorgonzola cheese, and olives in a balsamic dressing. Abigail enjoyed experimenting with recipes ranging from Taiwanese juicy dumplings to grilled salmon stir-fried with fresh mangoes, bell peppers, and white onions.

After years of daydreaming about owning a restaurant, Steve and Abigail finally decided to take the plunge and open one themselves. They had long conversations about what to name their restaurant, what kind of food they would serve, and where they would locate the restaurant. Steve's boss was surprised to receive Steve's resignation notice but wished him the very best with his new venture. Excited and nervous at the same time, Steve and Abigail got their business license, signed a lease for their restaurant, and got busy. Starting a restaurant was a lot of work. They had to purchase all the equipment, design the menu, and get exterior signage made. Steve spent a good portion of his days dealing with contractors and managing their work. Abigail utilized her art background to pick out the colors, décor, and theme of the restaurant. Every detail was carefully thought through and double-checked. They were exhausted at the end of each day, but Steve and Abigail knew in their hearts that they were making their dream a reality.

After many months of hard work and pouring over $300,000 into the space, Steve and Abigail were proud business owners as they stood in front of the camera during the ribbon-cutting ceremony put together by the local chamber of commerce. They hired two employees and couldn't wait until customers started pouring in. Abigail placed ads in various coupon books and magazines. Steve hired a web designer to build a website. Whenever she had time, Abigail went around the local community to hand out flyers and menus. Steve would man the restaurant and greet every customer who came in. After a long day at work, Steve would take care of the kids at night while Abigail stayed up late to keep the books and work on their taxes.

"How are we doing?" Steve asked Abigail one cool autumn evening after the restaurant had been open for six months. She looked through the books and said, "Well, we are still losing money every month, but that's true of all new businesses, right? I think we should stick through this tough period and things will pay off. Would you agree?"

Steve thought about the question awhile and then nodded. "Yeah, you're right. Let's stick with it."

Over the next few months, the restaurant got a little busier as more people learned of the restaurant and liked the food. Steve and Abigail were working harder than ever, and their restaurant finally went from losing money every month to turning a small profit. Although this was cause for celebration, Steve and Abigail felt more stressed than ever. The small profit from the restaurant was their only income. They had a mortgage payment, car payment, grocery bills, and two kids to support, and such a small profit was nowhere near enough to cover their living expenses. Every month, Steve and Abigail watched their retirement money and savings account get lower and lower.

After three years of running their restaurant, Steve and Abigail came to my office. They were thinking about selling their business and wanted to know how much it was worth. I analyzed their financial statements and examined their business operations. They told me that they had invested over $450,000 into this business venture. I wished I'd had better news for them, but their situation was dire. They both worked sixty hours a week and took home a total of $30,000 a year. The business was no longer losing money, but they just couldn't live on $30,000 a year. I hesitantly shared the truth with them that they would be lucky if someone bought their business for $60,000 with all equipment and fixtures included. It was not the answer they wanted to hear, but they knew that if they wanted to move on with their lives now, they would have to accept the losses.

At my business brokerage office, I run into sellers like Steve and Abigail all the time. Although the names of the people you read about in this book have been changed for confidentiality, Steve and Abigail's situation is actually quite common. Starting a business is a dream that many people have. What could be more romantic than striking out on your own, turning your passion into a business, and making your dream a reality? I do admire people who have the courage and stamina to start their own business, but the odds are stacked against them. It costs a lot of money to start a business—often double or triple what the entrepreneur might initially expect. It also takes a lot of time to start a business, and the entrepreneur may not have the time to get other sources of income. In the story above, of course, Steve quit his corporate job in order to run the restaurant. Once the business is up and running, there can be many months of losses. Very few start-up businesses end up turning a profit, and even fewer start-ups turn enough profit for the owners to live comfortably.

In my experience of meeting thousands of business owners and performing business valuations as well as my own experience buying and starting businesses, I've come to realize that starting a business from scratch is overrated. Starting a business from scratch may be romantic, but it is not romantic when people end up selling their business for pennies on the dollar. If you want to become a successful business owner in today's economy, there are six myths about business ownership that need to be dispelled.

Myth 1: If you want to own a business, you must start it from scratch. Laura was a very bright woman in her midthirties. Throughout her career, she had worked at several property-management companies, steadily moving up the ranks. In recent years, she had felt overworked and underappreciated at her company. After some confidential job searching and being offered a position, she'd left the company she had been with for twelve years. Her position with the new company was fresh and exciting at first. It allowed her to travel throughout the country, which she loved. After nine months at this new company, however, Laura had begun to feel unchallenged. It was a dream of hers to be a business owner, but she just didn't see how she could do that without losing the steady paycheck from her job.

When I spoke with Laura, she was in the process of getting another job. Her eyes lit up when I mentioned that my business brokerage office had just sold a profitable property-management company a few months ago. She would have loved to purchase such a company. Given her property-management background, she could have bought the business and really grown it to the next level. Her only regret was not knowing she could have bought a business instead of starting one.

Our media and popular culture can lead us to believe that being an entrepreneur means starting your own business from the ground up. So ever since I discovered the power of buying a business, I've made it my mission to educate as many aspiring entrepreneurs as possible that buying a business is often a smarter way to become an entrepreneur.

Myth 2: Buying a business is more expensive than starting one. This is perhaps my favorite myth. Many people tell me that they have to start a business from scratch because they don't have enough money to buy a business that is already successful. The truth is that it is actually more expensive to start a business than to buy one. Don't believe me? Let's think this through.

When you start a business, it can often be months before the business even opens its doors. In the case of Steve and Abigail, they worked hard for many months just to get the restaurant open. They not only had no income during that time but also were spending hundreds of thousands of dollars to get the restaurant ready. Once the restaurant opened, they had a different set of expenses. They needed to pay their employees. They needed to pay rent. They needed to spend money on advertising and marketing to get customers in the door. At the end of every month, they could only hope that their business income was enough to cover their business expenses. At the beginning, it is not uncommon for start-up businesses to experience one to two years of losses before breaking even and finally turning a profit. Once a business turns a profit, the question then becomes whether it is profitable enough. For example, was it worth it to Steve and Abigail to work sixty hours a week and make only $30,000 a year? Could their time have been better spent doing something else and making a higher return?

When you take into consideration all the start-up costs, customer-acquisition costs, and opportunity costs, it is actually cheaper to buy a business than it is to start a business. Think about it. Would you rather be Steve and Abigail, having spent $300,000 just to start the restaurant, suffered through a year of losses every month, and poured about $450,000 total into this venture in the last three years? Or would you rather be the buyer of their restaurant for $60,000 and inherit a business that has a modest following and reputation, with profits of $30,000 a year from day one and $300,000 worth of equipment that is only three years old? Not everyone wants to work sixty hours a week and make $30,000 a year, but starting from something and building it up to the next level is a lot easier than starting from nothing and needing to build something. My point is that, in most cases, it is more expensive to start a business than it is to buy one.

Myth 3: Whether you buy or start a business, the risks are the same. The reality is that starting a business is a lot riskier. The number one reason entrepreneurs go out of business is that the company runs out of cash. Why would a company run out of cash? The most likely reason is that the company's expenses are higher than its income, so there is a loss. When you read in the news about some large company losing several million dollars, it's probably just an abstract concept you don't think twice about. When you are running a small business, however, having a loss is a very serious thing. When you need to pay your employees, your rent, and your vendors, any shortfall you have is coming out of your personal checking account. If you don't put money into the business from your personal funds and it runs out of cash, your business is likely to meet its end.

It is a relief, let me tell you, that when you buy an existing business, it is profitable from day one. This assumes, of course, that you are buying a profitable business. If you were to buy an unprofitable business, chances are you wouldn't pay very much for it. Either way, your risks of buying a business are dramatically lower than the risks of starting a business.

Myth 4: You can own only one business because running it will take up all of your time. Owning only one business because you think that running it will take up all of your time is an outdated notion. People do that only because they don't know how to build enough profits, how to systemize the business, or how to let go. In today's fast-changing world, having only one source of income is risky. I am a huge believer in staying flexible and adaptable. By owning multiple businesses as a lifestyle business owner, I get to do what I want with my time, live a great lifestyle, and lower my vulnerability to economic cycles by owning businesses in different industries.

I know what I've accomplished may sound difficult, but let me assure you that it can be done. Every year, I work with hundreds of business buyers and help them find the right business to buy. You don't have to start with eight businesses. Start with one, turn it into a lifestyle business, and buy another business if you desire.

Myth 5: It's equally easy to become a lifestyle business owner whether you buy or start the business. I wish this myth were true. Unfortunately, I learned the hard way that it is much easier to become a lifestyle business owner if you buy a business instead of start one.

In my experience, there are too many things that need to be set up and established when you start a new business. Your business doesn't have enough history yet. What was working for you when you initially started the business may not be working right now. Customers don't know your business well enough yet. They may come to your business because it's new but slowly revert to their old habits as the novelty factor wears off. You may not hire the right employees to begin with, and it may take you some time to finally build the right team. When you start a business from scratch, expect it to take at least four years before you can become a lifestyle business owner. If you try to step back into the background before four years, too many things will be up in the air and you may quickly find yourself having to step into the business just to get things going again. It's also hard mentally to come back to the business after you take off. It's like taking a year off college and trying to come back to finish your degree. It's much easier to just stay the four years before trying to take off.

By contrast, it can take as little as one year to become a lifestyle business owner when you buy an existing business. How long it takes to become a lifestyle business owner will depend on the condition of the business you buy. If you buy one that is in disarray, it will take longer than a year before you can step back. But it is not unreasonable to see people who have purchased a well-run business become lifestyle business owners in one year.

Myth 6: It's equally easy to make good business decisions whether you buy or start the business. Vision is a funny thing. I am talking not about your eyesight but about your ability to dream of and see the future. People are often willing to spend a lot of money because they believe in their vision. Let me give you an example. My business brokerage firm represented a Mexican-grill franchise for sale. The owner had owned it for three years. The business had revenues of over $500,000 a year and was essentially breaking even. It wasn't losing money, but it wasn't making money either. The asking price was $100,000. After exposing the opportunity to thousands of potential buyers, I still didn't have anyone willing to make an offer yet.

But people were lining up all day long to become a franchisee of this exact same Mexican-grill franchise and putting in over $300,000 to start a brand-new location with no proven sales. Think about that. Would you rather spend $300,000 to start a brand-new location with no proven sales or spend $100,000 to buy the exact same franchise with $500,000 a year in proven sales? Whether it's logical or not, the truth is that people will often pay a lot of money for a dream. Maybe they think that if they spend $300,000 to start a brand-new location, they can make $1 million or $2 million a year! Who knows? But if they see the actual performance of an existing location, they are hesitant to spend $100,000 even if the business has $500,000 in proven sales and the equipment is only three years old.

The reason I share this story is that when you are starting a new business, it is actually harder than you think to make good business decisions. So much of what you do is driven by your vision and your passion, and people tend to make emotional decisions that turn out in retrospect to be bad for them financially. But when you take the route of buying a business, you are more likely to be logical. You will be evaluating the current financials of the business. Let's say you really love pets and want to own some kind of pet-grooming business. If you go the route of buying a business, you will probably think twice when you see the current owners of a pet-grooming business working sixty-five hours a week and making $20,000 a year. This is why I suggest that aspiring entrepreneurs buy a business before starting one. When you are buying a business, it is much easier to stay logical and make good business decisions.

Why Would People Sell Their Business?

Sometimes I am asked why a person would sell his or her business. There can be any number of reasons, but here are some common reasons I see:

- **Retirement**. I come across many business owners who have owned the business for thirty years, and it is time for them to retire. I love these businesses, because they are often very profitable and well established. These sellers are looking for the right person to hand the baton to—someone who can take good care of the business and take it to the next level.

- **Health issues**. Sometimes, the owner's health issues can create a motivation to sell the business. I always recommend being as sensitive and respectful as you can, because you don't want to come across as taking advantage of someone's need to sell due to poor health.

- **Relocation**. It is not uncommon for one spouse to run the business while the other spouse has a corporate job. If the spouse's corporate job requires moving to a different state, the couple may decide to sell the business.

- **Spending more time with family.** Many business owners don't know how to become lifestyle business owners, so they spend a large portion of their life working in their business. The desire to spend more time with their kids or the need to take care of an aging parent can motivate them to sell it.

- **Traveling the world.** Although most business sellers probably won't tell you of their secret desire to travel the world, this motivation (and variations of it) has to do with wanting to have more free time. I once represented the sellers of a medical supply business who hadn't taken a vacation in fourteen years. What they wanted more than anything else was to have some time off.

- **Tired of doing the same thing.** This happens more often than you may think. When I asked the owner of a profitable auto-repair shop why he wanted to sell his business, he said, "Aaron, I've been doing the same thing for thirty-six years. It's time for me to do something new with my life." People often get bored or feel unchallenged after doing the same thing for many years. A change of scenery is what they need in their lives.

- **Partnership dispute.** If the partners don't get along, selling the business and distributing the proceeds may be the way to settle a legal battle. Be careful if you are buying a business due to a partnership dispute, as the company may not be run well because of it. By the time you take over the business, revenues and profits could be much lower than they were before.

- **Divorce.** If the business owner is going through a divorce, selling the business may be part of the divorce settlement or just a way for the business owner not to be reminded daily of his or her ex. Going through a divorce doesn't always mean selling the business, but it certainly can be a motivation to sell.

- **Other business interests.** It is also quite common for the owner of a successful business to own multiple businesses. I once represented the seller of a manufacturing business who wished to dedicate more time to his other company. To him, that was a perfectly logical reason to sell his profitable manufacturing business.

- **Industry trends**. As I've said before, it pays to stay flexible and have multiple sources of income. If the industry trends become unfavorable for one of my businesses, I may consider selling it.

- **Lack of profits**. Unfortunately, this is more common than I would like to see. Many business owners just don't make enough money running their business and feel like their time could be better spent doing something else (such as getting a job). Buying a business that is not very profitable could be a great turnaround opportunity, or it could just be a lemon. I will share with you in the coming chapters how to tell the difference between the two, but just know that the lack of profits is often a motivation to sell.

- **Exit strategy**. Some business owners are planners who years ago planned to sell the business at a certain time. There isn't necessarily an external event forcing the business owner to sell. In this case, the exit has been planned way in advance.

By now, I hope you can see that there are a variety of reasons for people to sell their businesses and that buying a business is way smarter than starting a business. This is not to say that I never start businesses from scratch. But if this is your first time becoming a business owner, I would highly recommend buying a business. It is less risky, more profitable, and easier to become a lifestyle business owner by purchasing a business than by starting one from the ground up.

~ INVITATION TO ACT ~

What is your biggest takeaway from this chapter?

_____

_____

_____

_____

_____

_____

~ Free Training Videos ~
Visit www.LifestyleBusinessOwner.com
to download
your free training videos on
becoming a lifestyle business owner!

CHAPTER 5

What Kind of Business Can You Afford?

An eager young man came to my office one day. Let's call him Michael. He was excited to buy a business. He had $20,000 saved up, and he wanted to buy a business that would let him take home $500,000 a year. I politely gave him a reality check and explained to him how much money it really took to buy a business.

The encounter with Michael taught me that most people do not have a realistic understanding of how much money it takes to buy a business. At an intuitive level, you can know that highly profitable businesses are more desirable and therefore more expensive to buy. But how does the profitability of a business determine its sale price, and how do you figure out what size business you can afford based on the amount of cash you have? It is my intention in this chapter to clear the fog surrounding business valuations so you can understand how the sale price of a business is derived, whether the seller's asking price is reasonable, and what size business you can afford to buy.

As a business buyer, your first step is to figure out how much money you need in order to live. We would all love to make a million dollars a year, but I am

41

not talking about your dream number here. How much money per year do you really have to make? Is it $36,000 a year? Or is it $250,000 a year? When you buy a business, it will be your full-time job for the first twelve months. You will spend forty hours a week or more working at the business, learning everything you can, and gradually stepping back after twelve months once you've implemented the Lifestyle Business Owner Formula. You must have a realistic idea of the minimum amount of money you need in order to live. It might be nice to live on $100,000 a year, but you may find that after tallying up your living expenses, you really only need to make a minimum of $78,000 a year.

The next step is for you to understand how business valuation works for small businesses. Selling a business is not like selling a house. When you sell a house, the price it sold for becomes public record. When a privately owned business is sold, however, the sale price is usually confidential. In most cases, people don't even know that the business has been sold. Unlike public companies traded on the stock market, privately owned businesses have no disclosure requirements to the general public. Unless you work with someone such as a business broker who sells privately held companies for a living, figuring out how businesses are valued can seem like a mystery.

What you should understand is that business valuation for a big company is very different than for a small company. When you read in the news about some giant company buying another company for $2 billion, that number is really no indication of how much a privately held business is worth. If you think about it, ultimately the value of the business is how much the buyers are willing to pay. If the buyers think a company is worth a lot of money, then it is. If the buyers don't, then it is not. In other words, what potential buyers think is valuable matters a lot.

Let me give you an example. In 2006, Google acquired YouTube for $1.65 billion. Now, that's a lot of money. At the time of acquisition, YouTube had nowhere close to the revenues or profits to justify a $1.65 billion sale price. Why was Google willing to pay so much? In this case, what was valuable to the buyer was not YouTube's revenues or profits but its audience. In other words, Google couldn't have cared less whether YouTube was making money. What Google wanted was the views from the YouTube website, which fit into Google's long-term plan.

Of course, most people don't have hundreds of millions, or even a few million, to buy a large company. What we are talking about here is buying a small, privately held company that individuals like you and me can afford. To give you a sense of what I mean by a small company, I am talking about businesses that are worth $200,000, $500,000, or maybe even $2 million. Once you get into businesses that sell for many millions of dollars, the price becomes out of reach for most individuals.

Okay, so what do the buyers of these small, privately held businesses value? In most cases, the buyers of small businesses are people leaving their jobs and going into business for themselves. They have loved ones to support and bills to pay. In other words, they really need to be sure that the business makes enough money for them to pay their bills and support themselves and their families. To put it simply, how much money the owner makes determines the sale price of the business. If the owner takes home a lot of money, it is a valuable business to the buyers. If the owner doesn't make very much, the business can't be sold for much.

I am simplifying business valuation a bit here, but I cannot emphasize enough the most important factor in determining the value of a small, privately held business—the owner's income. You may have heard rumors about how companies can sell for two times or four times their revenues. The truth is that revenues don't matter that much. If a company has $1 million a year in revenues and $900,000 in expenses, the company may be showing a profit of $100,000 a year, but the buyer still needs to pay the bank using this $100,000 a year before he or she can take any money home. If a buyer were to pay $1 million for this business and put 25 percent down, the debt service alone could be $95,000 a year or more. No buyer in his or her right mind would pay $1 million for the business and take home only $5,000 a year. In other words, despite the company having $1 million a year in revenues, the company is not worth $1 million or some multiple of its revenues.

When it comes to valuing a small business, buyers care about the owner's income more than any other factor, so the market value of a small business can be determined mostly by the owner's income. The more income the owner makes, the more valuable the business is. In fact, we have a term in the business brokerage world known as owner's discretionary income, or ODI. Learning how to calculate the ODI of a business will give you a pretty good idea of how much a business is worth. Let me show you how this is done.

In order to calculate the ODI of a business, you will need the seller to provide you with some financials. In the world of small business, getting accurate books from the seller is often half the battle. Many sellers do not keep accurate financial records and may attempt to sell their businesses with few or no books. They may claim that they take home $100,000 a year, but they have nothing to back it up. If this is the case, don't walk, run! If a business seller comes to me with no books, I will share with him or her the unfortunate reality that the business value has been dramatically hurt because buyers will not be willing to pay very much for a company with no books.

When I talk about having good books, I mean having an accurate year-to-date profit-and-loss statement, a balance sheet, and at least two or three years of tax returns. If you are not used to reading financial statements, this process can seem a bit intimidating. But let's walk through it together, and you will see that the basic idea is not as complicated as it sounds.

Let's start with the profit-and-loss statement, sometimes called P&L for short. You may also hear it referred to as an income statement. It's all the same thing. The profit-and-loss statement tells you whether the business is generating a profit or a loss. The top half of the profit-and-loss statement shows you all the revenues of the business, and the bottom half shows you all the expenses of the business. When you total up all the revenues and subtract from it all the expenses, you end up with a net-income figure. If the net income is a positive number, the business made a profit; if the net income is a negative number, the business had a loss—hence the name profit-and-loss statement. It tells you whether the business is making a profit or not. Let's take a look at an example:

Profit-and-Loss Statement - January to December 2016	
Revenues:	
Revenue source 1	$400,000
Revenue source 2	$400,000
Revenue source 3	$200,000
Total Revenues	**$1,000,000**
Cost of Goods Sold	$400,000
Gross Profit	**$600,000**
Operating Expenses:	
Advertising	$120,000
Amortization	$2,000
Automobile expense	$16,000
Charitable contributions	$1,000
Depreciation	$4,000
Equipment rental	$2,000
Insurance	$4,000
Interest expense	$2,000
Laundry	$2,000
Licenses	$1,000
Office supplies	$1,000
Officer compensation	$80,000
Payroll expenses	$250,000
Rent	$60,000
Telephone	$2,000
Travel and entertainment	$6,000
Utilities	$4,000
Waste disposal	$1,000

Total Operating Expenses	**$558,000**
Net Ordinary Income	**$42,000**
Other Income	$200
Other Expense	$0
Net Income	**$42,200**

Let's see what this profit-and-loss statement tells us about our example company. In the year 2016, the company had three revenue sources. I didn't specify what the revenue sources were because they could be anything. Maybe the company made its revenue by selling TVs. Maybe the company made its revenue by selling magazine subscriptions. Maybe the company made its revenue by selling clothes. It doesn't matter. The fact is that the company had three different revenue sources, and when you total up the revenue generated by each source, the company had total revenues of $1 million for the year.

Now come the expenses. The expenses are shown in two places: cost of goods sold near the top and operating expenses near the bottom. As the name suggests, the cost of goods sold is cost directly related to the goods being sold. In other words, if the company sells TVs, the cost of goods sold is the amount the company paid to acquire the TVs. If the company sells clothes, the cost of goods sold is the amount the company paid for the clothes. If the company buys a TV from the distributor for $400 and resells it to the customer for $1,000, the company's revenue would be $1,000, and the cost of goods sold would be $400. The more TVs the company sells, the higher the cost of goods sold will be.

The second type of expenses are called operating expenses. Think of them as overhead expenses you need to spend just to keep the business running—things like insurance, rent, utilities, and so on. Know that accountants prefer to separate expenses into two categories (cost of goods sold and operating expenses), but for our purposes, they are just expenses. All we care about is that the company made $1 million in revenues and had the following expenses: $400,000 in cost of goods sold and $558,000 in operating expenses. If you take the total revenues of $1 million and subtract the cost of goods sold of $400,000, you end up with an intermediate number of $600,000, called gross profit. If you take the gross profit of $600,000 and subtract the operating expenses of $558,000, you end up with a net ordinary income of $42,000.

We are very interested in this number, the net ordinary income. If you take the net ordinary income number of $42,000, add any "other income," and subtract any "other expense," you will end up with the final number, called net income. In our example, other income amounts to $200. For our purposes, we don't really care about other income or other expenses. The definition of "other income" or "other expense" is that it doesn't usually happen during the ordinary course of business. Maybe the company got rid of some old desks and made a gain of $200. Selling desks is not what the company does, so the accountant classifies it as other income and puts it at the bottom. The point is that we are most interested in the net ordinary income figure (not the net income figure), because the effects of other income and other expense can usually be ignored.

Let's see where we've been. By reading the profit-and-loss statement, we have understood that after subtracting all the expenses from the total revenues, the company made a small profit (net ordinary income) of $42,000 in the year 2016. Now, here's the million-dollar question: does the number $42,000 truly reflect how much money the owner took home? You might be tempted to look at the profit-and-loss statement, go straight to the line called net ordinary income, and say, "Ha! The owner made $42,000 in 2016." Well, not so fast.

Before you declare that the owner made only $42,000 in 2016, let's look over the list of operating expenses one more time. If you look carefully at the operating expenses, you may notice a line called officer compensation for $80,000. What's that? Well, it's the salary the owner paid himself or herself. It was an expense to the business, but the owner received the benefits. So if we really want to know how much money the owner made, we've got to add the owner's salary of $80,000 to the profit of $42,000 shown on the books.

What we are trying to do here is to determine the owner's discretionary income, or ODI, of the business. What is the owner's true income? In the world of small business, many business owners like to make their net income look as low as possible (because it lowers their tax obligations). If a business owner spends $4,000 on a vacation in Hawaii that has nothing to do with the business, calls it a travel expense, and puts it as an operating expense on the company books, we've got to add back the cost of that trip when we are calculating the owner's true income.

The basic idea here is to calculate the owner's true income by taking the net ordinary income (which may be artificially low) and adding back all the expenses that are really for the owner's benefit. The following table shows some common expenses that are added back and the reasons why.

Expense to be added back	Rationale
Officer compensation	This is salary paid directly to the owner.
Travel expense	If this is the owner's personal travel that has nothing to do with the business, it can be added back.
Meals and entertainment	If the meals-and-entertainment expense has nothing to do with generating more income for the company and is more for the owner's personal enjoyment, it can be added back.
Charitable contribution	Donating to charity is usually discretionary. If the buyer buys the business and chooses not to donate to charity, the business will probably still run fine.

Depreciation	This is a book expense for tax and accounting purposes. If there is a depreciation expense of $2,000, the business owner hasn't cut anyone a check for $2,000 that particular year.
Interest	Most small businesses are sold free and clear, meaning that the seller will pay off all debt at closing. This means the seller's interest payments are unique to the seller and will not affect the buyer.
Amortization	Another book expense similar to depreciation.
Company benefits for owner	These can include company funds used for the owner's life insurance, the owner's retirement plan, the owner's health insurance, and so on.
Auto expenses	Some companies have legitimate automobile expenses (such as having a fleet of vehicles used for delivery). Legitimate automobile expenses cannot be added back. But if the auto expenses shown on the company books are for the owner's personal vehicles that have nothing to do with the daily operations of the business, then the auto expenses can be added back.

Using our example company from earlier, let's suppose the automobile expense is for the owner's personal vehicle that has nothing to do with the business operations. Let's also suppose all the meals, entertainment, and travel expenses are discretionary. Let's see, then, if we can calculate the ODI for this business:

Net Ordinary Income	**$42,000**
Add Backs:	
Amortization	$2,000
Automobile expense	$16,000
Charitable contributions	$1,000
Depreciation	$4,000
Interest expense	$2,000
Officer compensation	$80,000
Travel and entertainment	$6,000
Total Add Backs	**$111,000**
Owner's Discretionary Income (ODI)	**$153,000**

Once we take the net ordinary income of $42,000 from the profit-and-loss statement and add back the discretionary expenses we can find, we are able to conclude that the owner's discretionary income in the year 2016 was $153,000.

So what does this mean? What does an ODI of $153,000 tell us about the value of the business? ***As a rule of thumb, most small businesses sell for two to three times their most recent year's ODI.*** The sale price of a business is most heavily determined by its most recent year of financial performance. I like to also see at least two or three years of historical tax returns because I want to make sure that the company has an established history and that its revenues aren't all over the place, but for the business valuation itself, the most important year is the most recent one. Occasionally, a larger business or one in a unique industry may fetch a sale price four or even five times the most recent year's ODI, but the majority of small businesses do not get to this level. As a rule of thumb, think two to three times the ODI.

Within that range, the exact amount the business sells for depends on how desirable the business is. If the business is highly desirable, it will sell closer to three times its ODI. What makes a business highly desirable? Well, having a really high ODI would certainly make it especially desirable. The business being in a niche industry with few competitors can also make it desirable. In our example, is an ODI of $153,000 considered highly desirable? In my experience, it is middle of the road. Think of it this way. If you own the business free and clear, you would make $153,000 a year. But that's assuming you own the business free and clear. If you don't have enough cash and need to get a loan in order to buy the business, the loan payments could be as much as $45,000 a year. After paying the bank, you would have $108,000 a year to live on. How desirable is that? Taking home over $100,000 a year is not too bad, but there are businesses that allow the owner to make a lot more. In my experience, an ODI of $153,000 is in the middle of the desirability spectrum, so the business is probably worth 2.5 times its ODI, which comes to $382,500. In other words, the business will probably sell for around $400,000. If this same business was in an industry that was unique, with limited competition, it might sell for three times its ODI, fetching a sale price closer to $450,000.

If you are not entirely sure what multiple to apply, working with a business broker will be tremendously helpful. What I've shared with you is a general rule of thumb, and pricing guidelines vary from industry to industry. If you are looking to buy a larger business that lets the owner take home several hundred thousand dollars a year, the business broker might calculate EBITDA (earnings before interest, taxes, depreciation, and amortization) and price the business based on a multiple of EBITDA instead of on a multiple of ODI. Whether it is the ODI or EBITDA that is used, the basic principle is the same. We are recasting the financials to show the owner's true income and basing the sale price of the business on a multiple of that income.

Now that you have a general understanding of how the sale price of a small business is derived, let's talk about how much cash you need to buy a business. As of the writing of this book (in 2017), banks will lend you 75 percent of the purchase price. Sometimes you can negotiate with the seller to get him or her to lend you 15 percent of the sale price. In other words, you might be able to buy a business with as little as 10 percent down. I will give you an example. Let's say you are buying a business for $1 million. The bank will lend you 75 percent of the sale price, or $750,000, via an SBA loan. If the seller is not willing to offer any seller financing, then you would need to come up with the remaining $250,000. But if you manage to convince the seller to lend you 15 percent of the sale price, or $150,000, then you just need to come up with a down payment of 10 percent of the sale price, or $100,000.

Most small businesses are purchased with anywhere between 10 and 25 percent down, depending on whether the seller is willing to offer any seller financing. If negotiation is not your forte and you are wondering how in the world you would convince the seller to offer seller financing, working with a good business broker will be tremendously helpful, because business brokers deal with purchase and sale negotiations all the time.

Before we move on, let me address a few frequently asked questions.

Question 1: So I need 10 to 25 percent cash as down payment to buy a business. Where do I get the cash for this? Well, ideally you have the down payment you need in a savings account already. If not, there are companies that will allow you to finance your business purchase with your 401(k) or IRA as well.

Sometimes people sell other, less productive assets (such as a piece of land they inherited that isn't generating any cash flow) and use the money to buy a business that generates cash flow.

If you are really short on cash, asking friends and family for help is an option. Buying a smaller business that requires less cash is another option. Banks used to allow people to take out a home equity loan and use the money to buy a business. Since the Great Recession of 2008, however, banks are reluctant to do that unless there is someone else in the household with a job or another source of income that can support the loan payments.

Question 2: Other than the cash I need for the down payment, will I need extra cash for anything else? Yes. You will need some extra cash for operating capital. Depending on the nature of the business you buy, you may need an extra 10 percent of the purchase price of the business as operating capital or reserves to properly run the business. If you work with the right bank, the bank can finance much of the operating capital.

You will also need some cash for closing costs. Escrow fees usually range between $1,000 and $3,000 depending on the size of the business, and the cost is usually split fifty-fifty between the buyer and seller. There will also be some UCC search fees to check for liens on the business. The total cost for that is usually less than $200 split between the buyer and seller, so plan on at most $100. If the seller has on deposit with the landlord any security deposit or last month's rent, you will need to reimburse the seller for these amounts at closing. Also, some expenses may need to be prorated. For instance, if the seller has already paid rent for the entire month and closing takes place on the fifteenth of the month, the buyer needs to reimburse the seller for rent for the second half of the month.

Another common surprise that business buyers get is the amount of state tax they need to pay in cash at closing. The exact amount of tax you will need to pay depends on the industry of the business you are buying as well as where it is located. Every city and state have different tax laws, which is why it is important for you to work with a knowledgeable business broker, CPA, and escrow attorney who can educate you on the taxes you will need to pay.

Question 3: What if banks won't lend me the money? I am always a little wary if the banks are unwilling to lend money on a business. You see, the bankers are smart. They want to make sure they can be repaid. If they don't want to lend the money, it's due to either the business being a bad bet or you as the borrower being a bad bet.

Let's talk about the first scenario—the business being a bad bet. If you are buying a business with no books or one that's losing money, chances are the banks won't want to lend money on it. If the banks won't lend you the money (and the seller isn't willing to offer seller financing), that means you need to come up with 100 percent of the purchase price in cash. Many businesses that sell for $20,000, $40,000, or $75,000 are usually paid for using 100 percent cash from the buyer with no bank financing involved. Unless there is a really good reason for you to buy such a business, I usually encourage people to stay away from businesses that banks consider unworthy of funding.

The second scenario is that the bank thinks the borrower is a bad bet. Perhaps you have bad credit or items such as a bankruptcy or foreclosure on your records. When I lost my house during the Great Recession, it was a terrible mark on my credit report. All of my credit cards were canceled, and I had a really hard time getting loans from banks. But I did not let that stop me. When I found an opportunity to purchase a great business and property that had synergy with another business I owned, I asked all of my banker contacts if they knew of any lender that would work with people with bad credit. Finally, I was referred to one particular lender. The interest rate was higher due to my poor credit, but I got the loan approved.

Question 4: What kind of terms can I expect from an SBA business-acquisition loan? The best person to talk to is the banker, because lending conditions are constantly changing. If you want to know what kind of terms are being offered by banks, just call up several banks and ask them what they are currently offering.

As of the writing of this book (in 2017), here's what I am seeing in the marketplace. For someone with good credit, the interest rate for an SBA business-acquisition loan is somewhere around 2.75 percent + the Wall Street Journal prime rate. If the Wall Street Journal prime rate is 4 percent, then the interest rate on your loan would be 6.75 percent. The bank will finance 75 percent of the purchase price, and the loan is amortized over seven to ten years. If you are buying both the business and the property, some banks may be able to lump the business and property together and give you one loan amortized over a longer period of time.

The borrower usually puts 25 percent down. At the very minimum, the buyer puts 10 percent down, the seller finances 15 percent of the purchase price, and the bank finances 75 percent of the purchase price. If the seller is financing a portion of the purchase price, the bank may require no payment be made to the seller for two years. This is a sticking point for a lot of sellers. You are asking the seller to lend you 15 percent of the purchase price, but the bank will not allow you to make any payments to the seller for two years. Interest can accrue during this time, but you are not allowed to make payments to the seller for two years. After two years, how soon you can pay the seller off depends on the cash flow of the business. The seller may want you to pay off everything in one lump sum as soon as the two-year mark is up, but the bank may not allow that because it could hurt the cash flow of the business too much and thus jeopardize your ability to pay the bank. Depending on the particular situation, many banks want to see no payment to the seller for the first two years; after two years, you will begin paying off the seller over five years with something like a 6 percent interest rate.

Whenever you are getting an SBA loan, all the business equipment will need to be used as collateral for the loan. If you own a house, your house will also need to be used as collateral for the business loan. This is a surprise for some buyers because they were hoping not to have to use their personal house as collateral for the business loan. Before the Great Recession of 2008, banks were much more lenient on this point. Unfortunately, many banks got into trouble during the Great Recession, so they are a lot stricter today. If you don't own a house, you won't need to offer a house as collateral for the SBA business-acquisition loan. But if you own a house or rental property, the bank will require you to use your property or properties as collateral.

If you are getting an SBA loan, plan on the process taking sixty days to close. Don't say to the seller, "I am getting an SBA loan for 75 percent of the purchase price, and I want closing to take place next week." Once you submit all the required information to the bank (such as the loan application, your personal financial statement, three years of personal tax returns, your résumé, proof of funds for the down payment, history on the business you are buying, three years of tax returns on the business you are buying, and so on), the bank will usually give you a yes or no within seven to ten days. If it's a yes, the bank will give you a checklist of items to accomplish before closing. Completing this checklist will take some time. The bottom line is: plan on forty-five to sixty days to close if you are getting an SBA loan to buy the business.

A final word on banks: it is highly important to choose the right bank to fund your business acquisition. There are a lot of banks that tend to give lip service and drag the process out for months. Even worse, they may drag the process out for months and then deny the loan after all that wait. I tend to like small banks that are eager to fund business-acquisition loans. Through experience, I have collected a network of good bankers I work with. If you work with a good business broker, he or she can often recommend banks that can get the deal done fast.

Bringing It Together

Okay, we've covered a lot of ground in this chapter. We've talked about how much cash you need to buy a business, how to calculate the owner's discretionary income (ODI), and how the ODI relates to the sale price of the business. Let's see if we can bring everything together using an example.

Let's say you have $140,000 cash to buy a business. Right off the bat, let's take $40,000 and set it aside because you may need the cash for closing costs, taxes due at closing, lease security deposit, reserves, and so on. That leaves you $100,000 to use as a down payment. To be on the safe side, let's assume the seller won't offer any seller financing. That means we are looking at a scenario in which you are putting down 25 percent and the bank is lending you 75 percent of the purchase price. Thus, in our example, you can buy a business with a sale price of up to $400,000 (since 25 percent of $400,000 is the $100,000 cash you have).

What kind of businesses sell for $400,000? Remember, the rule of thumb is that most small businesses sell for two to three times their ODI. If the business is not very attractive (that is, the ODI is low), a multiple of 2 is used. If the business is highly attractive (that is, it has an ODI in the several hundred thousands of dollars a year or it's in a niche industry with few competitors), a multiple of 3 is used. In our case, let's assume the business is somewhere in the middle, so we are using a multiple of 2.5. For you to pay $400,000 for a business, the owner should make $160,000 a year (since $160,000 times 2.5 equals $400,000).

If you own this $400,000 business free and clear, you would make $160,000 a year. But you do not own it free and clear. In our example, you are putting down $100,000 and borrowing $300,000 from the bank. Let's say the bank is lending you the $300,000 at an interest rate of 6.75 percent amortized over ten years (or 120 months). If you go online and search for "amortization calculator," you will find a number of websites that allow you to calculate your monthly loan payment. In our case, the amortization calculator will tell you that your loan payment comes to $3,444.72 per month. Multiplying your monthly loan payment by twelve months gives you an annual loan payment of $41,336.64.

Now comes the verdict. Your business generates $160,000 a year in ODI, and you will spend $41,336.64 of your ODI paying the bank, which leaves you with a cash flow of $118,663.36 per year. Can you live on $118,663.36 per year? If the answer is yes, then congratulations! It is very possible for you to take your one-time investment of $140,000 cash and buy a productive business that generates a cash flow for you of $118,663.36 year after year after year. In case you are wondering what your return on investment is, dividing $118,663.36 by $140,000 gives a whopping 85 percent return. That is amazing compared to the 0.1 percent you get from a savings account or the 5 percent you get from rental real estate! Even your best stocks that perform at 10 percent year after year can't beat the 85 percent return from buying a business.

I hope by now you can understand my excitement for buying good businesses. If you like cash flow, you can usually get dramatically higher cash flow by buying a well-run, privately owned business than by buying rental real estate, investing in stocks or bonds, or putting money in the bank. In our example, in which you have $140,000 cash, you can get $140 a year in interest by putting it in a savings account returning 0.1 percent, get $5,600 a year in dividends by buying a stock with a 4 percent dividend yield, get $7,000 a year in cash flow by buying a rental property with a 5 percent return, or get $118,663.36 year after year by buying a well-run, privately held business that gives you an 85 percent cash-on-cash return.

Granted, buying a good business successfully takes training, education, and experience. But can't the same thing be said of becoming a successful stock investor or real-estate investor? If you like having lots of cash flow, consider learning how to buy a good business, because buying a business produces way better cash flow than any of the other options does.

⊨─────────────────────────⊨

~ INVITATION TO ACT ~
What is your biggest takeaway from this chapter?

_____

_____

_____

_____

_____

_____

~ Free Training Videos ~
Visit www.LifestyleBusinessOwner.com
to download
your free training videos on
becoming a lifestyle business owner!

⊨─────────────────────────⊨

CHAPTER 6

Getting into the Right Line of Business

If you have ever bought stocks, you'll know that you can make money just as easily as you can lose money. If you have ever bought rental properties, you'll know that you can make money just as easily as you can lose money. Buying a business is no different—you can make money just as easily as you can lose money. It is my intention for this chapter to show you how to pick a good business to buy.

People often come to me and start asking questions such as, "Where do I find businesses for sale? Do I go online? Do I write letters to business owners asking if they want to sell? Do I talk to a business broker? How do I find a good business broker?" Although these are excellent questions, asking them at this point is getting a bit ahead of yourself. Once you know how to look for businesses for sale (which I will show you how to do in the next chapter), you will find more businesses for sale than you can imagine. If you do not have an understanding of what a good business looks like, you may end up feeling overwhelmed by all the choices available or be seduced into buying a business that isn't in your best interest. For this reason, I am adamant about my students being able to articulate what a good business is. Before you ever go out to search for businesses for sale, you need to be able to clearly state what a good business looks like and what the right kind of business is for you.

Okay, so where to begin? A good place to start is by looking at your background, experience, and interests. Earlier, I shared with you the story of Laura, who had spent many years working in the property-management industry. She had a lot of experience in this field and wanted to stay in it. She just wanted to be her own boss and not be an employee anymore. In her case, buying a property-management company seemed like a perfect fit.

But not everyone's situation is so clear. Not everyone wants to stay in the same field. Perhaps you daydream about owning a particular type of business. Or perhaps you just want to be a lifestyle business owner and want to know the type of business that will give you the best chances of becoming one. Whatever the case may be, I want you to know that you can buy a business in your current field if you want, but you don't have to. I have seen business buyers succeed either way.

Let me speak to those of you who may be daydreaming about owning a particular type of business. Although I cannot read your mind, I can share with you a pretty common scenario I run into. There are people who would love to own a business that happens to be their hobby. For instance, let's suppose you love flowers, so you decide to buy a flower shop. When the business you own is also your passion, it can sometimes be difficult to make the hard choices. In order to stay in business, the business owner needs to apply logical decision-making that includes making profits as a top priority. When the business is also the owner's passion, emotions can sometimes get in the way, and the necessary hard choices may not match the owner's artistic vision. This might lead to the business losing money, and any business that is unprofitable for a prolonged period of time loses its appeal. In the worst-case scenario, the business owner might stop enjoying the hobby because it gets associated with the negative business experience.

In my experience, some of the most successful business buyers are those who buy a business for the purpose of making money; they keep their personal hobbies separate. You can be passionate about business ownership, financial freedom, and time freedom. You can be passionate about providing a great work environment for your employees and about your business making the community better in some way. You do not necessarily have to be passionate about the product or service. A garbage collection service might be an extremely profitable and desirable business with a steady and secure stream of cash flow, but not many people are passionate about the act of garbage collection. Finding meaning and purpose in your life is hard enough. Finding a profitable business that also gives your life the unique meaning and purpose you are looking for is doubly hard. I am not saying you should never turn your passion into a business, but I suggest keeping an open mind when you are looking for a business to buy, evaluating each opportunity on the merits of the business itself, and not ruling out a business purchase simply because you are not passionate about the product or service.

So what are some guidelines when it comes to choosing the best business to buy? Well, buying the right business starts with being in the right industry. You can buy the most well-run business in a dying industry and find yourself going out of business as the industry dies. For instance, you probably don't want to be in the typewriter-repair business in the twenty-first century.

The next thing to understand about industries is that not all industries are equally profitable. Some industries are really cutthroat, while others are much easier to own a profitable business in. Sometimes I see business owners doing everything right in terms of running their business yet still struggling with a lack of profits. As much as we'd like to attribute our success or failure to our personal efforts, sometimes it is just a reflection of the greater industry environment that is beyond anyone's personal control. That's why being in the right industry is often half the battle.

So what's a good industry to be in? A lot of people are attracted to the retail industry. This is understandable, because, after all, retail businesses are common and easily understood. There are lots of retail businesses everywhere we look, whether they're selling clothes, jewelry, or vacuum cleaners. In my opinion, however, unless the product is in a very specialized market, retail businesses are terrible to buy. Here's why. As a small-business owner, you are competing against all the big retailers, including Walmart, Home Depot, and other big retailers that carry the same products you do. The big retailers can get a lower cost on their products due to their volume, which means they can afford to sell the products at a lower price than you can. In the retail industry, customers can easily compare apples to apples. They can either buy the product from you or from a big retailer at a cheaper price. In the retail industry, you are largely competing on price, and in that realm, small businesses just can't win. For this reason, retail business owners can't charge too much for their products (since their prices are already higher than the prices at the big retailers), making it difficult to achieve high profit margins in the retail industry.

The service industry, though, is an industry in which it is more difficult for customers to compare apples to apples. For instance, let's say two businesses offer auto-repair services, and one business charges more. Will customers choose the cheaper option by default? Not necessarily. In fact, many customers would choose to get their cars repaired at a shop they feel they can trust, a shop with friendly and knowledgeable staff members that offers great service. In other words, it is possible for business owners in the service industry to charge premium prices by offering excellent customer service. For this reason, small-business owners in the service industry are often able to achieve profit margins of 15 to 20 percent, whereas those in the retail industry might achieve profit margins of only 10 percent. Want an extreme example? Just think about haircuts. There are businesses that offer to cut your hair for $20, and businesses that offer to cut your hair for $300. The patrons of the salon that offers the expensive haircuts will swear that a $300 haircut is just not the same as a $20 haircut. Again, the beauty of the service industry is that it is harder for customers to compare apples to apples, allowing you, if you do things right, to charge premium prices without a corresponding increase in costs.

There are other industries you can choose from—manufacturing, wholesale, distribution, and technology, just to name a few. Many of these businesses can be attractive to business buyers, but they are generally larger in size and therefore more expensive to buy. Some of these businesses may require specialized knowledge in order to properly run the business if there is not a large enough staff to manage the technical aspects of the business. For instance, if a software company relies heavily on the owner as the main programmer, I probably wouldn't want to buy the business if I am not a software programmer. But if the software company has an established staff and the owner doesn't do any programming, I may consider buying it.

Personally, I like business operations that are simple to understand—businesses that can be run by anyone with good business and management skills without needing heavy industry knowledge. The reason is that I am interested in being a lifestyle business owner. I want to be able to step back, work few hours, and let the business run by itself for the most part. If the business is too complicated and relies too heavily on specialized industry knowledge, the owner or owners will have a hard time stepping back. I like the service industry a lot because most service businesses are simple enough to manage and profitable enough to allow a manager to be hired, so the owner can step back.

The restaurant and food industry is highly popular, so I want to say a few words about that. As a business broker, I have seen the financials of thousands of restaurants. Unfortunately, most of them are suffering financially. I am not saying you can't own a profitable restaurant, because I have seen some of those too. But for the most part, owning a restaurant is highly competitive, and any industry with lots of competitors is hard to be profitable in. Many restaurants I see also struggle with employee theft. Owning a successful restaurant is possible, but it's one of those industries that I recommend the buyer having been in before.

Personally, I like niche industries that most people have never heard of. The fewer people know an industry exists, the fewer competitors there are. I once sold a laundry service that specializes in washing cloth baby diapers. The business delivers clean cloth diapers to the customers' doorsteps once a week, picks up the dirty diapers, and washes them at the company's facility using specialized industrial washing machines. The business is very profitable, and the operations are so simple to understand that anyone with good management skills can run it. In fact, the seller had previously been a banker. Customers love using this service because it is cheaper than buying disposable diapers, healthier for babies, and better for the environment, preventing thousands of disposable diapers from going into the landfill. Some of the best businesses I've seen are niche businesses that most people never think about.

One of the most common mistakes people make when buying a business is falling for what I call *glamour*. Some businesses are more glamorous and romantic than others. For instance, what could be more romantic than owning your own restaurant in the perfect location? Can't you just smell the food? Owning a flower shop is quite romantic too. Just look at those beautiful flowers! Don't they smell good? Unfortunately, all that glitters is not gold. In my experience, the more glamorous the business is, the less profitable it tends to be. When I look at business owners who make a lot of money, they are the people who own companies that service septic tanks, collect garbage, or wash baby diapers. They're not exactly sexy or glamorous, but they are profitable businesses that offer a steady income stream and a great lifestyle for the owner. Obviously, not every business needs to be disgusting or dirty in order to be profitable, but some alarm bells should be ringing if you come across a business that is glamorous, dazzling, and romantic. I often tell my clients, "See that glamorous business over there? The owner is probably working sixty hours a week and making $30,000 a year. See that guy who owns a big house on the lake? He's the one who owns a septic-pumping business."

Something else to consider is how recession-proof the business is. Some businesses, such as those in the construction industry, are terribly cyclical. When the economy booms, construction companies do really well. But when the economy tanks, construction companies can really go bust. Some people have a greater tolerance for risk than others, but I personally prefer businesses that offer more or less a steady income stream whether the economy is up or down. Obviously, no business is 100 percent recession-proof, but some businesses are more recession-proof than others. For instance, people get sick regardless of the economy, so businesses in the health-care field are more likely to have a steady stream of customers, even during a recession. People need to file taxes regardless of the economy, so a bookkeeping service or accounting service tends to have a steady stream of income year after year. There are many people who love their pets and take good care of their pets even during a recession, so a business that caters to pet owners may be more recession-proof as well.

What trends do you notice in our country? What do you see happening around you? Paying attention to the overall trends in society can clue you into businesses that will stay profitable for years to come. For instance, the baby boomers make up such a huge portion of the American population that industries have boomed and busted according to the age of the baby boomers. When the baby boomers were babies, the baby industry boomed. When they reached adulthood, the housing industry boomed. Now, the baby boomers are reaching retirement. They are selling their big houses, downsizing to smaller houses or apartments, and planning for their golden years. Businesses that cater to this large, aging population, whether they offer retirement planning, health care, or upscale travel, may do well.

A question I am often asked is whether it is a good idea to buy a franchise. Well, there are pros and cons to doing so. With a franchise, you get a proven business model, systems, training, and a recognizable brand name. But you also have the ongoing expense of a franchise royalty fee. In many cases, the franchise royalty fee is equivalent to the salary of an operations manager. In other words, it can be more difficult for franchise owners to become absentee business owners, because money that would otherwise be used to hire a general manager, which would allow the owner to be more hands-off with the business, instead must be used to pay the franchise royalty fee. Unless you own multiple franchises, you may need to be an owner-operator at your business day in and day out if you choose the franchise route. Something else to consider is that owning a franchise is similar to still having a boss telling you what to do. Some people like it; some don't.

That's why another aspect to consider is your personality. Just because a business is right for someone else doesn't mean it is right for you. The Myers-Briggs Type Indicator assessment, known as the MBTI, measures your psychological preferences in how you perceive the world and make decisions. It is a tool used by more than 10,000 companies, 2,500 colleges and universities, and 200 government agencies in the United States. Understanding the basics of the MBTI can point you in the right direction when it comes to buying a business:

1. *Extraversion (E) vs. Introversion (I).* If you are an extravert and enjoy networking, buying a business in which you get to do a lot of selling, cold-calling, or networking might be right for you. Extraverts recharge their batteries by being around lots of people, so having lots of social interaction is important. Introverts, however, might consider buying a

business with a sales team already equipped. Buying a business such as a mailbox store where customers come in might also be more suited for introverts than buying a business in which the owner needs to make cold calls or perform outside sales. Introverts are good at developing deeper relationships with fewer people, whereas extraverts are good at developing weaker relationships with lots of people. Given this, introverts might consider purchasing businesses that have fewer clients and making up the revenue by making sure each client is a well-paying one.

2. *Sensing (S) vs. Intuition (N)*. People with a preference for sensing like to rely on facts, whereas those with a preference for intuition are dreamers and visionaries. Both are important to the success of a business, since seeing only the facts but not the possibilities, or vice versa, can hurt the full potential of a company. A sensor and intuitive might consider partnering together to buy a business. Short of partnering, an intuitive might want to hire a sensor during the due diligence process to be grounded on the facts, whereas a sensor might want to hire an intuitive as an advisor to see the growth and expansion possibilities of a business.

3. *Feeling (F) vs. Thinking (T)*. Feelers tend to be sensitive and nurturing and can do very well in businesses that require a good amount of empathizing and nurturing. Examples might include a spa business, daycare center, or wellness supplement store. But thinkers tend to be more detached, logical, and direct. Thinkers might enjoy owning businesses that are highly logical, such as a bookkeeping service or investment-advisory firm, and being in roles that allow them to be direct with others.

4. *Judgment (J) vs. Perception (P)*. People with a preference for judgment are planners. They tend to be very organized. They make plans in advance, set milestones, and execute their plans. People with a preference for perception, however, tend to go with the flow, make decisions on the fly, and be good at staying open and responding to whatever comes. People with a preference for perception might enjoy an entrepreneurial environment in which lots of ambiguity exists, things are constantly in flux, and choices need to be revised again and again based on feedback. In

contrast, people with a preference for judgment might consider buying a franchise or a larger business with established systems in place so they can make plans, create budgets, and know what to do at all times.

As you can see, choosing the right business to get into is a holistic decision that takes into account not only the greater industry trends but also your personality. When you see a business that interests you, how do you make sure it is a good business? Here are fifteen things to analyze when you come across a business that interests you:

1. *Revenues.* The annual revenue amount gives you an idea of the size of the business. Revenues that are too low may indicate a business that is too small for your goals, and revenues that are too high may indicate a business that is out of your budget. Personally, I do not like to buy businesses with annual revenues under $1 million. I learned the hard way that businesses with annual revenues under $1 million are just too small and not set up well enough yet, which means that it takes a lot of effort to grow the business to the point at which a manager can be hired and the owner can become a lifestyle business owner. Don't get me wrong; it can be done, but it usually takes longer and requires more financial investment to get the revenues up.

2. *Number of Units Sold.* Is this a high-volume, low-margin business? Or does the business make a few very expensive sales? Knowing the number of units sold or the number of jobs performed can help you understand the business model.

3. *Average Price of Units.* How does this compare to the industry in general? Are their prices on the low end, middle end, or high end of the market? Let me give you an example that ties together points one, two, and three. Let's say I am analyzing an auto-repair shop for sale that has annual revenues of $1 million. That's good, because I want a business doing at least $1 million a year in revenues. My next questions would be: "How is this $1 million a year in revenues achieved? What is the number of units sold and the average price of the units?" In our auto-

repair example, the number of units sold means the number of cars fixed. The average price of the units means the average size of the repair ticket. Let's say the auto shop fixes, on average, seventy-seven cars per week, and the average repair order is $249.75. You can do the math and check that seventy-seven cars per week times fifty-two weeks per year times a $249.75 repair ticket comes out to $1 million per year in revenues (with a little bit of rounding involved). So what does this tell you? Well, having seventy-seven cars to fix a week tells you how busy the shop is. Having lots of customers lowers my risks, because if I lose a few, I am still okay. What about the average repair order amount of $249.75? Well, some repairs are more expensive than $249.75, and some are less expensive. We are talking about the overall average achieved by the shop. Suppose you learn that auto-repair shops in this region are all charging prices that lead to an average repair order amount of $450. That would tell me that this shop is undercharging its customers, and there is very good potential to buy the business, raise prices a small amount, and still be okay. It may also tell me that the current service advisor is not proactive enough with upselling and service recommendation efforts and may need additional training or even need to be replaced.

4. *Gross Margin and Markups.* What is their gross margin and markups, and how do they compare with the industry average? A lot of industries have guidebooks and publications that tell you what the industry average is and what the various financial ratios should be. Comparing the performance of the company to the industry average can tell you a lot. If you are unsure of how to find the industry average, working with an experienced business broker can be very helpful.

5. *Profit Margin.* At the end of the day, what is the company's profit margin? A low profit margin may be a bad sign, indicating that the industry is tough to be in. Or it might be a value-add opportunity if the average profit margin for the industry is much higher and the seller simply has operating expenses that are too high.

6. *Owner's Discretionary Income (ODI).* Ultimately, you care about the ODI because it is income discretionary to the owner. It is income you

can use to pay yourself, meet your loan payments, or hire a manager and step away if there isn't a manager in place already. As explained in the previous chapter, the value of the business is directly linked to the ODI, so calculating the ODI of the business will also tell you if the business is overpriced.

7. *Number of Employees.* Knowing the ratio of the number of employees to annual revenues and comparing this ratio to the industry average can give you an idea of how efficiently the business is run. A business that is too lean might experience employee burnout and high turnover, and a business that is not lean enough has a payroll that is too high.

8. *How Much Employees Are Paid.* Knowing the compensation structure of the staff can help you gauge the competitiveness of the business with that of other employers.

9. *Current Owner's Marketing Methods.* How are current customers finding out about the business? Knowing how the business is currently marketing itself can give you clues about the expansion potential of the business. If the seller puts hardly any effort into marketing, it could be a good sign, because once you buy the company, you can really increase business by becoming proactive with marketing.

10. *Size of Customer Base.* A business with a lot of customers is more diversified, and therefore a lower risk, than a business that depends on a few high-paying customers for most of its revenues.

11. *How Well Customer Records Are Kept.* Does the business keep good records? Having good customer records, such as e-mail addresses, phone numbers, and home addresses, will allow you to send additional promotional offers to the existing customers.

12. *Expansion Potential.* How great is the expansion potential? How easy would it be to grow this business? What opportunities do you see that the seller may not be taking advantage of?

13. *Position Relative to Competition.* How many competitors are there for this business? How easy is it for new competitors to enter the market? What is the competitive advantage of this business, and how easy is it to copy?

14. *Location of the Business.* Depending on the industry, the location may play an important role in the success of the business. If the business is a mobile handyman service, the exact location of the company office is not that important. If the business is in retail, however, having a good location can be very important.

15. *Trends in the Last Three to Five Years.* What trends can you see in the last three to five years? Is the business trending up, staying the same, or trending down? What about the overall trend of the industry? Is the industry growing, staying the same, or declining? What about the area? Is the area growing, staying the same, or declining?

This is by no means a comprehensive list, but it is a useful starting point for business buyers to evaluate opportunities that suit their goals. If you are feeling overwhelmed by all the information I've thrown at you, know that you do not have to do this alone. Buying a business successfully is a team effort. You make the final decision, but you have various team members to support you. A business broker can notify you of potential opportunities. A mentor can help you evaluate those opportunities. A CPA can help you verify the financials. An attorney can help minimize your liability. In the next chapter, I will show you exactly how to build a great team and how to buy a business from start to finish.

~ INVITATION TO ACT ~
What is your biggest takeaway from this chapter?

_____

_____

_____

_____

_____

_____

~ Free Training Videos ~
Visit www.LifestyleBusinessOwner.com
to download
your free training videos on
becoming a lifestyle business owner!

CHAPTER 7

Buying a Business from Start to Finish

s I mentioned in the last chapter, buying a business takes a great team. If you try to do everything yourself, you can easily feel overwhelmed or end up making a poor choice. With a competent and knowledgeable team in place, however, buying a business can be both profitable and fun.

At this point, many people say to me, "But, Aaron, isn't hiring all these advisors expensive? I don't really want to spend all that money!" I can relate to this. When I was younger, I didn't see the need for good advisors. I thought they were expensive (especially the good ones), and I tried to do without them. Unfortunately, I ended up making some business mistakes that were even more costly than the fees I was "saving." Looking back, I would have been much better off if I had hired those advisors in the first place.

Not all advisors are created equal, of course. I want to show you which advisors are essential, which ones are secondary, and how to recognize a good advisor when you see one. Shall we begin?

Essential Advisor 1: Business Broker

When you are buying a business, having a good business broker on your team will save you a lot of time and potentially costly mistakes. The buyer of a carpeting and flooring business once hired me to represent him as his business broker. At one point, we were sitting in a meeting with the seller, the seller's landlord, and my client—the buyer. Once the business was sold, the seller would no longer be the tenant. The buyer of the business would become the new tenant that leased the space. We were sitting in this meeting, and my client was negotiating the lease with the landlord. I could clearly tell that what my client was saying was making the landlord feel increasingly uncomfortable. I understood where my client was coming from, but I knew that if he continued to push his point, he would go too far. I stepped in and explained to my client that what he was asking for was unreasonable. I could see the relief in the landlord's face, and we ended up working out a new lease that was beneficial for all parties. The landlord later called me and thanked me for my negotiation skills, because he felt it was really going in the wrong direction. Had I not been there, the buyer might have pushed the landlord away, ended up being rejected as a potential new tenant, and lost an opportunity to buy a great business.

A good business broker should not only notify you of potential opportunities but also guide you every step of the way. The seller's business broker represents the seller. As the buyer, you may want your own business broker to represent you. Here are ten things to look for when choosing a business broker:

1. *Specialty.* There are brokers that specialize in selling houses, brokers that specialize in selling commercial properties, and brokers that specialize in selling businesses. As a business buyer, you don't want a broker who mainly sells houses or commercial properties. Does your broker specialize in selling businesses?

2. *Track record.* How many businesses has the broker sold? Is the broker experienced in the process of helping people buy a business?

3. *Financing contacts.* Does the broker have good relationships with key SBA lenders? Does the broker have intimate knowledge of which banks to use for which types of business transactions? The broker's ability to

help you obtain good financing in a timely manner can be the difference between the deal's success and failure.

4. *Choice of escrow.* Which escrow company does the broker use? Does the escrow company specialize in business-sale closings?

5. *Marketing package.* How does the business broker present the business to potential buyers? Is the broker organized in getting you the information you need to make a purchase decision? The marketing packages prepared by my business brokerage can sometimes be several hundred pages long, giving potential buyers extensive information to make an informed purchase decision.

6. *Confidentiality.* What actions does the broker take to ensure that confidentiality is maintained? The failure to maintain confidentiality of the sale can cause the deal to fall apart. Employees should not find out that the business is for sale until the day after closing when the seller introduces the employees to you as the new owner.

7. *Minimizing liability.* What actions does the broker take to minimize any potential liability?

8. *Minimizing tax obligations.* Does the broker understand the tax implications of purchase price allocations for both the seller and buyer? Is the broker proactive in working with your CPA to help you minimize your tax obligations?

9. *Straightforward communication.* You want a broker who is honest and open with you and is not afraid to tell you the truth—even if it is hard to hear. If you are asking for something unrealistic, you need a broker who can keep you in check. Ultimately, you need to ask yourself, "Is the broker specialized, experienced, and sincere?"

10. *Business ownership experience.* Working with a business broker who has personally bought businesses before and has made those businesses successful is recommended over working with a business broker who is a mere salesperson. You want a successful entrepreneur advising you on a good business to purchase, not a mere salesperson who is looking to earn a commission.

Essential Advisor 2: Business Mentor

If this is your first time buying a business, I would definitely recommend hiring a business mentor. There are lots of life coaches and business coaches who do great work but may not have the business experience you need. What you need is a business mentor who understands how to buy a business, how to evaluate business opportunities, and how to make sure the business you buy aligns with your background, interests, and goals. You need a business mentor who has the experience to take company revenues and profits to the next level and understands the ins and outs of becoming a lifestyle business owner. My company offers various programs that give you the mentorship and support you need to buy a business and successfully become a lifestyle business owner.

Essential Advisor 3: CPA

Buying a business has tax consequences, so your CPA needs to be part of your team. When you buy a business, the purchase price will need to be allocated among several categories for tax purposes. Your CPA can explain to you what the tax consequences are and can suggest a purchase price allocation that is beneficial to you.

As a business buyer, you will most likely not want to buy the business in your personal name (because doing so exposes you personally to all the potential business liability). Chances are you will want to set up an entity to buy the business, and your CPA can be invaluable in helping you decide what kind of entity to set up so your taxes can be minimized.

How do you choose a good CPA? You don't want a CPA who only does your taxes once a year and never talks to you otherwise. You want a CPA who is proactive rather than reactive. You want a CPA who sits down with you and says, "Hey, let's map out a tax strategy for you for the short-term and for the long-term. How can we plan ahead together so we are proactively minimizing your taxes in the future?" A good CPA should talk to you in November or December every year to do some year-end tax planning. You see, by the time January comes around, it's already too late to make changes to last year's taxes. Before the year is over, your CPA should sit down with you, look at what you've done this year, calculate your tax liability, and suggest proactive actions you can take before December 31 so that when tax season comes around, you've already done everything possible to ensure your tax liability in the previous calendar year is minimized.

Essential Advisor 4: Business Attorney

There are many specialties in the field of law. In this case, you want a business attorney who is familiar with asset protection—someone who can work with your CPA to determine the best entity to form to buy your business. It is usually the attorney's job to set up the entity properly, prepare all the bylaws, properly issue the stock certificates, and correctly prepare the meeting minutes. There are companies that charge as little as $99 for incorporation, but I would not recommend them because you get what you pay for. Not doing everything properly can lead to your corporate veil being pierced, effectively losing you the asset protection your entity is supposed to provide. Hiring an attorney to be your registered agent and maintain your annual minutes is more expensive than doing it yourself, but it is worth the peace of mind.

A good business attorney can also help you in the negotiation process. If the seller wants to put an unfamiliar clause into the purchase-and-sale agreement, your attorney can explain its legal implications to you. Keep in mind, however, that you as the entrepreneur need to make the final decision. From the attorney's point of view, he or she is hired to protect you from potential liability. Buying a business carries some inherent risks—even the wisest possible business purchase carries some risk. If the business you buy on your attorney's advice fails, leading you to sue the attorney for failing to protect you, this is obviously not a good outcome for your attorney. Therefore, he or she is incentivized to be as conservative as possible. At the tiniest sign of danger, the attorney may advise you to back out—the unspoken logic being if you don't buy a business, you won't be doing anything risky.

Having a great business attorney on your team is essential, but keep things in perspective. I've seen inexperienced buyers let their attorneys scare them into inaction. Don't let your attorney become the entrepreneur instead of you. Listen to your attorney's advice, but make your own final decision. If you are not sure whether your attorney is raising a legitimate concern or just being overly cautious, seek advice from your business mentor.

Secondary Team Members

Once you have found one or two of your essential advisors, the rest should come pretty easily. A good business broker can refer you to a good CPA, who can refer you to a good attorney. Your secondary team members are usually found the same way—through referrals. By secondary team members, I don't mean that they are less important in any way. What I have intended to do is to put a framework around which team members you need first and which ones come later. The essential advisors are the ones you need first. Without a business broker, you won't have a business to buy. Without a business mentor, you may lack the guidance you need. Without a CPA and attorney, you may end up making a poor choice. These are the team members you need to gather first.

The secondary team members will naturally follow. You need to buy insurance, so you will need an insurance broker. If you are getting a loan to buy the business, your broker can suggest bankers to talk to. If your business has employees, you will need to hire a payroll-processing company. If your business accepts credit cards, you will need a credit-card processor. You may decide the website of the business is outdated; if so, you'll need a web designer. The list of secondary team members can go on and on, but don't worry too much about finding all of these secondary team members in advance. Your goal is to find one or two good essential advisors. Once you do, the rest of the essential advisors and secondary team members will follow.

Business-Buying Process

Now I am going to walk you through buying a business from start to finish. Step one is to find one or two good essential advisors—maybe a good business broker and business mentor. Interview a few people and pick the one you like. Once you have found one or two essential advisors, they can refer you to the rest of the essential advisors and secondary team members.

Once your essential advisors know that you intend to buy a business, it's time to search for potential opportunities. Since most business sales are conducted confidentially, you won't find For Sale signs in front of businesses. Your business broker will alert you to opportunities that fit your criteria. There are also a number of websites that advertise businesses for sale in a very generic way. You will know that a certain business is for sale in a general geographic area, but you won't know the business name or address until you sign a nondisclosure agreement. Some of these websites include BizBuySell.com, BusinessesForSale. com, BusinessBroker.net, BizQuest.com, and DealStream.com.

Once you find a business for sale that piques your interest, the next step is to sign a nondisclosure agreement, or NDA for short. You will probably be asked to sign an NDA for every listing you are interested in, because just about every business seller doesn't want his or her employees, customers, and competitors to find out that the business is for sale. Before you can see information such as the business name, address, and historical financials, you will be asked to sign an NDA. This is normal, so don't be alarmed if you are asked to sign a lot of NDAs as you look at lots of listings.

Once the NDA has been signed, you will be given the details on the business. How much detail you receive depends a lot on the seller and the seller's broker. At my business brokerage, when we represent the seller we like to put together confidential business reviews that can sometimes reach several hundred pages long. This way, potential buyers have all the information they need to make an offer. If you are lucky enough to receive a comprehensive information package, you can get to work analyzing the business using the metrics I outlined in the last chapter. If the information you receive is minimal, you will need to ask your broker (who will in turn ask the seller's broker, who will in turn ask the seller) for the exact information you need. At a minimum, you want to see the most recent twelve months of profit-and-loss statements so you can calculate (with your broker's help) the ODI of the business. Once you know the ODI, your broker and business mentor can help you determine an appropriate offer price. You will also want to see a few years of tax returns in order to verify that the numbers on the profit-and-loss statements are not just the result of someone typing whatever numbers he or she wants into a computer.

You will also want to understand the business operations. Arrange a conference call or in-person meeting with the seller if possible. I prefer in-person meetings because building rapport with the seller is important. If he or she thinks you are a better fit for the employees and the future of the company, the seller may end up selling the business to you even if he or she receives another offer that is higher than yours. You can also arrange a site visit to the business, although it will most likely take place after business hours because making sure none of the employees find out about the sale will be extremely important to the seller. Actually, it is important to you, too, because you don't want the employees getting scared and quitting before the closing date.

While we are on the subject, let me say a few words about the fear of employees quitting. If the employees find out about the sale and have months to stew about it before the new owner comes on board, they may secretly look for other jobs in case they don't like the new owner. The key to a successful business purchase is to make sure the employees don't find out about the sale until the day after closing. When you come on board as the new owner, the seller will introduce you to the employees and the employees to you. In all the years I've been selling businesses, I have found that having employees quit at this point is actually rare. Sure, there might be employees who quit later if they really can't get along with the new owner, but in most cases, the employees are more afraid of losing their jobs than you are of losing them. The key is to be positive and to assure the employees that you really value them, you want to learn from them, and you want to continue running the business the way it's been run. And that's the truth. Even if you intend to make changes to the business, you really should not do so right away. You don't know the business well enough yet. You don't know the employees well enough yet. After you've bought the business, the learning curve can take at least several months. During that time, all you are doing is learning how the seller ran things; you are keeping things exactly as they are. Any changes you make in the future should come gradually. If you do it right, the employees will appreciate you and stay with you. If they don't, you will have gained enough confidence in your ability to run the business and know what kind of replacements you need that you can fill the position with confidence.

Once you have gained a basic understanding of the business operations and seen enough financials to determine the value of the business, it is time to make an offer—assuming you want to proceed to that step. You can ask your attorney or your broker to draft the offer for you. If you ask your attorney, chances are he or she will draft an offer that is buyer friendly. Next, the seller will ask his or her attorney to review the offer, and that attorney will cross out a bunch of things to make it more seller friendly. Then your attorney will make a bunch of changes again, followed by the seller's attorney making a bunch more changes. Pretty soon, with all this back and forth, both you and the seller may be faced with pretty hefty legal fees.

In my experience, it is important to utilize attorneys the right way in order to get the advice you need without spending a fortune. To determine how much attorney involvement is appropriate, you need to know how much risk you are taking. There are essentially two basic ways to buy a business: asset sale or stock sale. Let me explain. Let's say you are buying a private security service called Ultimate Bodyguard. As you know, business owners usually don't like to operate businesses in their own names because it can expose them personally to all the potential business liability. Therefore, chances are that Ultimate Bodyguard is not owned in the seller's personal name but by the seller's corporation. Let's say Ultimate Bodyguard is owned by the seller's corporation, which is called Smith Enterprise Inc. Follow me so far? The seller is a shareholder of Smith Enterprise Inc., and Smith Enterprise Inc. owns Ultimate Bodyguard.

When you buy the company Ultimate Bodyguard, you can do it two ways. If you buy it via an asset sale, it means you will set up your own corporation to buy the business. Let's say you set up a new corporation called Anderson Enterprise Inc. In this case, Anderson Enterprise Inc. will buy Ultimate Bodyguard from Smith Enterprise Inc. In other words, you are buying the *assets* of Smith Enterprise Inc. Before the sale, it was Smith Enterprise Inc. doing business as Ultimate Bodyguard. After the sale, it is Anderson Enterprise Inc. doing business as Ultimate Bodyguard. The name of the business, along with all of the business's assets, is transferred from Smith Enterprise Inc. to Anderson Enterprise Inc.

Let's contrast this with a stock sale. In a stock sale, you are literally buying the stocks of the seller's corporation. Before the sale, the seller owned 100 percent of Smith Enterprise Inc. After the sale, you become the new 100 percent shareholder of Smith Enterprise Inc. It is still Smith Enterprise Inc. doing business as Ultimate Bodyguard. Only the shareholders of Smith Enterprise Inc. changed.

Why is this distinction between an asset sale and a stock sale important? It is important because even though you are buying the exact same company, you are taking on different amounts of liability. To put it simply, a stock sale is riskier to you as the buyer. Who knows what kind of questionable business Smith Enterprise Inc. has engaged in during all of its existence? If someone sues Smith Enterprise Inc. in the future and learns that you are the new shareholder of the corporation, guess what? You are liable for any potential liability the seller might have incurred in the past because the seller doesn't own the corporation anymore—you do.

When you buy the business using an asset sale, however, you are starting with a clean slate, so to speak. You just formed Anderson Enterprise Inc., so you know your corporation has a clean past. If people want to sue the seller, they sue Smith Enterprise Inc., which is still owned by the seller. Ideally, you want to buy a business using an asset sale because you don't know whether the seller's corporation has a clean past or not. Buy a business using a stock sale only if you absolutely must. There are times when a stock sale is the only way you can buy the business, whether that's due to licensing requirements, a major customer contract, the seller's tax consequences, or other reasons. There is a place for stock sales, but most small businesses are sold using asset sales because it limits the buyer's liability.

Now we can come back to our discussion about using attorneys. If you are buying the business using a stock sale, consult your attorney as much as you can because stock sales are riskier for the buyer. If you are buying the business using an asset sale, you can be a little more relaxed because, for the most part, you are buying only the seller's assets and not the seller's liabilities. How much you use an attorney should also be a reflection of the size of the transaction. If you are buying a $100,000 business, is it worth spending a fortune on attorney fees? Probably not. But if you are buying a $1 million business, is it worth spending several thousands of dollars on attorney fees? Probably.

Here are some tips to help minimize the attorney fees when you are making an offer. If you are doing a stock sale, don't open with a full-blown, multipage purchase-and-sale agreement. If you ask your attorney to draft a twenty-page purchase-and-sale agreement to submit as your initial offer, the seller's attorney will spend a lot of time editing those twenty pages, and then your attorney will need to spend a lot of time making counteredits. Before you know it, both you and the seller will have spent thousands and thousands of dollars on attorney fees. Instead, ask your business broker to draft a simple, nonbinding letter of intent, or LOI, that is one to two pages long. The LOI is a simple document that spells out the terms of the purchase: What is the purchase price? When is the closing date? What kind of noncompete agreement do you want from the seller? What kind of training do you want from the seller after closing? Use the LOI as your initial offer. The seller can usually respond to the LOI without getting an attorney involved, because it is just a matter of agreeing to the terms of purchase. Once the buyer and seller agree on all of the terms and finalize the LOI, then the LOI can be passed to an independent attorney (such as the escrow attorney) who doesn't represent the seller or buyer. That attorney can turn the short LOI into a full-blown, twenty-page purchase-and-sale agreement. Notice that a neutral attorney prepares the agreement. Why? Because you don't want any of the language to be one-sided. Once the full-blown purchase-and-sale agreement is ready, each side's attorney can review it and make minor changes if necessary. Hopefully not too much editing will be needed, though, since all the terms have already been agreed on and the purchase-and-sale agreement wasn't one-sided to begin with.

With an asset sale, things are even simpler. You can usually skip the LOI altogether. Your business broker should belong to some kind of local commercial brokers' association. In the world of selling houses, real-estate brokers belong to a local Multiple Listings Service, or MLS. The MLS allows the real-estate brokers to see what listings are available and also provides templates for making offers. The same thing is true for business brokers. Just as there is an MLS for residential properties, there is a different MLS for commercial properties and business opportunities. The commercial MLS is a local association that allows the business brokers in that area to see what listings are available and provides fill-in-the-blank templates for making offers. My point is that if you are doing an asset sale, your business broker can usually just fill in the blanks for you and put the terms you want into the purchase-and-sale agreement template provided by the commercial MLS. The reason these purchase-and-sale-agreement templates are pretty good is that they are designed to be neutral. You see, buyers' brokers use the commercial MLS as much as sellers' brokers do, so the MLS templates have already been reviewed by hundreds of attorneys on both sides. Why reinvent the wheel when there is already a tried-and-true purchase-and-sale-agreement template in place? When doing an asset sale, start your offer with a fill-in-the-blank, full-blown purchase-and-sale agreement provided by the local commercial brokers' association. If your attorney or the seller's attorney wants to make minor edits, that's fine. But the bulk of the purchase-and-sale agreement should be ready to go already.

Whether you start your offer with a simple letter of intent and later convert it to a full-blown purchase-and-sale agreement or start with a full-blown, fill-in-the-blank purchase-and-sale agreement from the local commercial brokers' association, there are some common elements in every offer. Here are some of the elements you may want to put into your offer:

- *Name of the buyer.* Are you buying the business in your personal name or in the name of a corporation or LLC? If you will be using a corporate entity to buy the business but don't have it set up yet, you can put your personal name for now, but you should add the words *and/or assigns* after your name so that you can later assign the purchase-and-sale agreement from your personal name to your entity. For instance, the name of the buyer would read *John Smith and/or assigns.*
- *Purchase price.* How much are you buying the business for?
- *How the purchase price will be financed.* Will you be getting a bank loan? Will you be asking the seller to offer seller financing? Or will you simply put up 100 percent of the purchase price in cash yourself so there is no bank loan or seller financing needed?
- *Financing contingency.* If you are getting a bank loan, you will want to say, "If the bank offers me XYZ terms, then I won't back out." For instance, "If the bank offers to lend me 75 percent of the purchase price at an interest rate that is 6.5 percent or less, amortized over seven years

or longer, then I won't back out due to bank financing." This is for the seller's protection so the seller understands exactly what "satisfactory bank financing" means to you. Your broker can help with this section.

- *Details on seller financing.* If you are asking the seller to provide some financing, you will want to state the terms you are asking for. Your broker can help with this section.

- *Feasibility contingency.* This is the amount of time you have to check over all the books and records of the business and conduct any inspections to ensure you want to proceed with the purchase.

- *Earnest money.* This is the amount you will send to escrow to communicate to the seller that you are serious in the event your offer is accepted. For business sales that are $1 million or less in purchase price, it is typical to see buyers putting down $5,000 to $10,000 in earnest money. Most offers contain at least the financing contingency and the feasibility contingency. If you waive your financing contingency because you are happy with the terms of the bank loan you got, waive your feasibility contingency because you are happy with your inspections of the business, and back out before closing, you will lose your earnest money. If the closing happens successfully, the earnest money is simply applied to the purchase price. In other words, the financing contingency and feasibility contingency are the two outs you have without losing your earnest money. You can add in more contingencies, such as, "If my partner doesn't like what she sees, then I can back out." The more contingencies you add, the more outs you have—but the weaker your offer is and the less likely it is to be accepted by the seller.

- *Closing date.* When do you want closing to take place? Most sellers want closing to take place as soon as possible, but you need to be realistic. Maybe it will take you thirty days to properly conduct all the inspections you want. Maybe it will take the bank sixty days to fund the loan. If there is a special license required to operate the business, maybe the license transfer will take ninety days. Set a realistic closing date for all parties to shoot for.

- *Noncompete agreement.* With the seller having intimate knowledge of the business, you certainly don't want the seller to start another business right next door to compete with you immediately after selling the business to you. The noncompete agreement is usually defined by a time frame and a radius. For instance, the seller can't compete with you for five years within a twenty-five-mile radius. It may be tempting to make the noncompete agreement as broad as possible (that is, the seller can't compete with you for fifteen years within a 150-mile radius), but keep in mind that the broader the noncompete is, the less enforceable it becomes in court. The noncompete agreement should reflect the nature and size of the business you are buying. If you are buying a trucking company for $3 million, a reasonable noncompete agreement will certainly be broader than would the noncompete agreement if you were buying an auto-repair shop on the street corner of a local town for $200,000.

- *Training from seller.* This may surprise you, but most of the transactions I see at my business brokerage contain a training period of two weeks. Can you properly learn from the seller how to operate the business in two weeks? In most cases, the answer is yes. If the seller is not a good trainer, you won't learn much more even if he or she agrees to train you for four weeks. In my experience, the quality of the training is more important than the quantity. To ensure you receive the seller's best efforts in training you, you may stipulate in the offer that a portion of the seller's funds will be held back at escrow until escrow receives a notice from you saying you are satisfied with the training. I am not saying you are limited to two weeks of training. In larger transactions, the seller may be very agreeable to sticking around for 90 days or 180 days. Sometimes I see a two-phase training process, beginning with an intensive, forty-hour-per-week training for two weeks and followed by occasional phone consulting (up to two hours a month) for twelve months. The exact details will vary, but be sure to stipulate some kind of free training by the seller in your offer so the seller will train you at no charge after closing takes place.

- *Franchise transfer fee.* If you are buying a franchise, the franchisor may charge a franchise transfer fee. Be sure to stipulate who pays this fee. Usually, the buyer is required by the franchisor to pay the franchise transfer fee.

Once you submit your offer, the seller will either accept it or come back with a counteroffer. There may be a few rounds of negotiations back and forth, and your business broker can help you tremendously throughout this process.

Once you have a fully accepted offer, a number of things need to take place. You need to send the earnest money to escrow. If you are applying for a bank loan, you need to put in your bank loan application. You need to set up your entity. You need to conduct your due diligence inspections to make sure you want to proceed with the purchase. You need to be introduced to the landlord, because you will become the new tenant after the business is sold. The landlord will either grant you a new lease or assign the seller's existing lease to you. The terms of the lease will need to conform to the bank's requirements if you are getting a bank loan. You will need to work with your business broker and CPA to allocate the total purchase price among several categories (such as equipment, goodwill, noncompete agreement, inventory, and so on) for tax purposes. You will need to obtain insurance, set up credit-card processing, and engage with a payroll-processing company. You will need to open your business bank account, get your business licenses, and set up accounts with vendors. You will need to obtain a reseller permit if the business buys products at wholesale and sells them at retail. If you are buying a franchise, you will need to get approved by the franchisor and attend the training offered by the franchisor. Throughout this whole process, you will need to keep track of the important dates:

- When is the date of mutual acceptance? This is the date the offer is fully signed around. Many other dates in the offer are calculated based on this date.
- When do you need to deliver the earnest money to escrow by?
- When do you need to agree on the list of assets not included in the sale (if any)?

- When do you need to agree on the allocation of the purchase price with the seller?
- When do you need to waive your feasibility contingency?
- When do you need to waive your financing contingency?
- When is the closing date?

As you can see, there will be plenty to do between the time you have an accepted offer and the time of closing. I know the list of to-dos can seem overwhelming. The key is to gather great team members who can help you throughout this process. Start the preparation process early. If you know you will be applying for a bank loan, check your credit score and fix any mistakes that might appear on your credit report. Update your résumé, gather the last few years of your tax returns, and take stock of your income, expenses, assets, and liabilities; the banker will ask for these items. Arrange your schedule accordingly. Searching for the right business to buy takes time. Once you find one, making an offer and negotiating the terms take time. Once the offer is accepted, working through all the items that need to be done prior to closing takes time. And once closing takes place, the training with the seller starts and you will be running the business full-time.

Congratulations! You've now bought your first business! Take a breath, congratulate yourself, and celebrate. Buying a business is a lot of hard work, but remember why you are doing this. Sometimes it can be easy to lose sight of the big picture when you are busy doing all the things that need to get done. That's when it helps to remind yourself of the reasons you work so hard to become a lifestyle business owner someday. In the next section, I will show you how to take the profits of the business you've bought to the next level. See you there!

~ INVITATION TO ACT ~
What is your biggest takeaway from this chapter?

_____

_____

_____

_____

_____

_____

~ Free Training Videos ~
Visit www.LifestyleBusinessOwner.com
to download
your free training videos on
becoming a lifestyle business owner!

PART III

How to Increase Profits

Lifestyle Business
Owner Formula

3 Empower your people

2 Increase profits

1 Buy a good business

CHAPTER 8

Increasing Revenues through Smart Marketing

We are now on step 2 of the Lifestyle Business Owner Formula. Step 1 is to buy a good business, and step 2 is to increase its profits. By buying a good business, you already have a tremendous head start over those who start a business from scratch. While those who start businesses from scratch are still struggling with losses month after month, your business is already profitable—you are just trying to take your profits to the next level. While those who start businesses from scratch are still trying to figure out how to get their first customers, you already have a database of existing customers you can market to. As I've said before, it's much easier to start from something and build it to the next level than it is to start from nothing.

At this point, you may be asking, "Aaron, I just bought a business. Why can't I jump directly to making the business run without me?" There are two main reasons. The first reason is that the seller is an owner-operator. Let's say the seller works at the business every day. If you hire a general manager to take over most of the seller's duties, there may not be enough owner's discretionary income (ODI) left for you to pay your personal bills. The second reason is that even if the seller is already a lifestyle business owner and works minimal hours at the business, you still need to learn the ins and outs of the business you've just bought. You see, confidence in being a lifestyle business owner derives from the ability to jump back in and fix things if needed. If you have no idea how to fix something if it goes wrong, you won't feel very secure being a lifestyle business owner. That's why I recommend every business buyer work full-time at the business for at least twelve months. I don't care if the seller worked only ten hours a week. After you've bought the business, you need to be there forty hours a week. I want you to learn as much as you can. Learn from the seller. Learn from the employees. Learn from the customers. Only when you've learned every little detail of the business will you acquire the confidence to step back later.

Your initial goal for the first few months should be to keep things the way they are and learn as much as you can. Even if you disagree with how the seller ran the business, I do not recommend making changes right away. If you make changes too quickly, the employees may get scared. You need time to gain the trust of your employees and show them that you care about their well-being. What's more, you may find that as much as you disagree with how the seller ran the business, the way the business has been run has been proven to generate X amount of revenues and Y amount of ODI. Before you try to make changes, at least gain the knowledge of what the seller did to generate those revenues and that ODI. There will be a time to implement changes to increase the ODI of the business, but the key is to make changes gradually rather than doing it too soon and too fast.

At this point, I want you to develop a concrete idea of how much you need to increase your ODI by in order to become a lifestyle business owner. Let's say you've bought a landscaping-service business in which the seller works fifty hours a week. What are the seller's job duties? Let's say the seller spends his time driving out to the customers' houses, giving out quotes, closing the sale, managing the employees, and overseeing the financial aspects of the business—and the business currently generates $100,000 a year in ODI. In other words, if you were to own the business free and clear, you would take home $100,000 a year as an owner who works fifty hours a week.

But you want to become a lifestyle business owner and work only five to ten hours a week. How much will you need to increase your ODI by in order to make that happen? Let's walk through the calculation. If you own the business free and clear, you would take home $100,000 a year. If you don't own the business free and clear but instead got an SBA loan to buy the business, your loan payments are (for example) $24,000 a year. So after paying the bank, your take-home cash flow has gone down from $100,000 a year to $76,000 a year. Now you want to hire a manager to take over the duties of giving out quotes, closing sales, and overseeing the employees. You will still monitor the business and work five to ten hours a week, but the manager will be able to take over many of the day-to-day duties that were previously performed by the seller. Let's say it costs $55,000 a year to hire a quality manager in your industry. If you were to hire this manager now, your take-home cash flow would be reduced from $76,000 a year to $21,000 a year. Can you live on $21,000 a year? Most people would rather not try. Remember, however, that you will be working only five to ten hours a week at the business. Let's say you want to make $80,000 a year while working that same five to ten hours per week. That means you need to increase your ODI from $21,000 a year to $80,000 a year—a $59,000 increase per year. That's your goal for the next twelve months. Buy the business, learn everything you can in the first few months, and start implementing changes gradually to increase your ODI by an extra $59,000 annually, at which point you can hire a manager and gradually step back.

Increasing your ODI by $59,000 (or whatever your desired dollar amount is) may sound difficult, but it's actually not as mysterious or complex as it may seem. There are only two ways to increase your ODI: increasing revenues and lowering expenses. You will likely need to do both. There are four skills to master if you want to increase your revenues and lower your expenses: engage in smart marketing, build a great team, make your operations run smoothly, and employ sound financial management. It is my intention to teach you these four skills over the next four chapters. Right now, we are going to start with smart marketing.

So you've spent two weeks training with the seller and learned what the seller is or is not doing with marketing. Which of the current marketing activities should you continue? Which of them should you stop? What new marketing activities should you start? To answer these questions, we need to learn what smart marketing is.

Smart marketing is improving your customers' experience and perception of your business from start to finish. Here's a strategy I've taught only to my exclusive coaching clients until now: think about your customers' current experience with your business from start to finish. To make the example more concrete, suppose you own an auto-repair shop in Boston. How do your customers know that they need your service? Do you remind them on a regular basis to bring their cars in for a checkup and regular maintenance, or do your customers think about needing auto-repair service only when their cars break down?

Once the customers realize that they need an auto-repair shop, how do they find your shop? Do they go online? Do they use smartphones? Is your website mobile-friendly? Does your website come up on the first page of Google's search results when people type in "auto repair Boston"? What other ways do customers find your shop? Do you have good signage? Does your building need a new coat of paint to stand out?

Once the customers find your shop, does it look credible? Are your online reviews positive? Are you affiliated with organizations customers trust, such as AAA? Does your shop exterior look clean and sharp as opposed to dirty and dilapidated?

Once the customers decide to do business with you, how is their actual experience? Does the person on the phone sound courteous, knowledgeable, and trustworthy? How is the customer's wait time compared to the wait time at other repair shops? How is the waiting experience? Are the chairs comfortable? Is there free Wi-Fi? Is the bathroom clean? Do employees storm in and complain to each other when customers are waiting in the lobby?

Once your customers leave, how do they feel? Do you have systems in place to wow them in some way every time? Do you thank them for doing business with you? Do you give them an incentive to become a repeat customer? Do you ask for their feedback? If you receive negative feedback, do you handle it constructively or say to yourself that this customer is crazy?

As you can see, marketing is how customers perceive you from start to finish. What can you do to improve that perception? When I bought my auto shop, I had a suspicion that the seller, who worked at the front counter, wasn't being very friendly to the customers. I remembered meeting him across the street and saying to him, "You know, I am seriously considering either buying your business or buying an HVAC company. Why should I buy your business?"

The seller became offended and yelled at me, saying, "Aaron! I know nothing about the HVAC company! Why would you ask me that?" I was taken aback by his response. I was a very serious buyer, and he had been trying to sell his business. If he was rude to me, I figured that he was probably rude to the customers as well. You see, when you buy a house and see something negative, it's a mark against the house. But when you buy a business and see something negative, it can often be an opportunity to improve the business and increase your sales or profits after you buy the business. In my case, noticing that the seller might not be very nice to the customers became an opportunity for me. After I bought the business, I made sure that everyone who worked there was friendly to the customers. In fact, I even put up a banner on the building that read, "New Owner. Friendly Service." Within one year, revenues increased by over 65 percent. I became a lifestyle business owner after one year, but revenues continued to grow. By the end of my second year, revenues had more than doubled what the seller had been generating for sixteen years previously. I am not trying to impress you with my story but to impress on you that smart marketing works. Following are five common mistakes people make when it comes to marketing.

Mistake 1: Thinking that advertising equals marketing. Advertising and marketing are very different things. There are many ways to market your business, and advertising is only one way to do so. In fact, advertising is often the most expensive way to market your business. If you think advertising is the same as marketing, you have just limited yourself to using only the most expensive way to market your business. There are lots of ways to market your business that are cheaper and more effective than advertising.

Lifestyle business owners understand that marketing is how customers perceive your business. This perception is influenced by the advertising materials you send out, but it's much more than that. How customers perceive you is also influenced by, among other things, how courteous your employees are, how they answer the phone, how clean or messy your store is, how quickly you respond to your customers' concerns, and the quality of the work you do for your customers. Everything that affects the customers' perception of you is marketing.

As you can see, advertising is only one component of marketing. Successful advertising brings customers to your door, but whether customers stay with you is another matter. You can make big claims in your advertising and bring lots of customers to your door, but if you cannot service them well, your marketing is not successful.

Want a marketing tip right now that has nothing to do with advertising? Talk to a handful of your customers and ask them about their overall experience. What is the most dissatisfying thing about your service? Their answers will tell you exactly what you need to do to improve.

Mistake 2: Thinking that effective marketing must be expensive. When you become a small-business owner, you will be approached by all sorts of sales reps who want you to advertise in their coupon book, magazine, or website. These sales reps are usually paid on commission—the bigger ad you buy, the more they get paid. In other words, they may try their very best to convince you that if you want your business to be successful, you should buy the most expensive ad possible.

I am not against advertising, and I do spend money on advertising. But I am very conscious of the fact that spending more money on advertising doesn't necessarily lead to more business. The most effective advertising may not be the most expensive advertising. Often, delivering the right message in the right way to the right people at the right time produces better results than simply buying the most expensive ad possible. Keep in mind that, many times, finding the advertising that works well is a bit of a trial-and-error process. Try something for at least three months to give it a fair shot, and avoid signing long contracts in case the advertisement doesn't produce enough results to justify the costs. I also understand that advertising is only one small component of marketing. Thinking about how I can improve my customer's perception of my business from start to finish will generate many ideas that will lead to more business, many of which will cost little to no money to implement.

Mistake 3: Giving up the responsibility of marketing. As a small business owner, you have a small budget and you need to watch your expenses carefully.

As tempting as it may be to hand over the task of marketing to someone else, many small businesses can't afford to put a marketing person on payroll. It's also difficult to outsource marketing to a marketing company or ad agency, because many of these companies are used to working with larger budgets. If you let an outside marketing company handle your marketing for you, you could end up spending tens of thousands of dollars on ideas that may or may not be effective.

I recommend that small-business owners learn some basic marketing skills. You can hire people to help you with various tasks, but you need to be the head of marketing. For instance, you don't have to be the one making posts on your company's Facebook page, but you need to be in charge of the social-media strategy and decide what's worth doing and what's not. If you want to become a lifestyle business owner, you need to master the art of marketing yourself. Only when you've mastered the art of marketing can you tell which ad is worth buying and which ad is not. Only when you've mastered the art of marketing can you decide what you need or don't need from an ad agency or marketing guru. Only when you've mastered the art of marketing can you confidently run your business knowing that you have the skills to bring customers and sales to your company.

Even after you've become a lifestyle business owner, you will still be working a minimum of five hours a week. I do not recommend spending zero hours a week on your business, because you need to monitor it and ensure that things are running smoothly. Guess what will be part of your job duties during those five hours a week? That's right. You will be getting feedback from your customers and employees, looking over financial statements, evaluating the effectiveness of your marketing, and deciding what you should continue doing, what you should stop doing, and what you should start doing. In other words, you are still the head of marketing even after you've become a lifestyle business owner. If you are not good with marketing, it's time for you to commit to mastering the art of marketing.

Mistake 4: Thinking you must engage in social media because it's *the* thing. Whether you need social media depends on what your business does and who your customers are. If you produce component parts for heavy-industrial manufacturers, your customers probably don't care about your Facebook page. They want quality component parts at competitive prices that can be produced to meet their volume requirements within the time frame they need. If you run a real-estate agency selling homes, however, having a social-media presence is important.

My point is that social media gets a lot of hype, and it may seem like every business needs an extensive social-media program. The truth, though, is that social media is only a piece of the overall picture. Remember what marketing is. How do your customers perceive your company from start to finish? Focus on designing a great experience for your customers from start to finish. Social media may be a part of it, but it's only a part.

Mistake 5: Thinking that marketing is constant. As much as we may want things to stay the same, the fact is that things change. The way customers behave changes. Let me give you an example. The Yellow Pages used to be a big deal. I remember sales reps who would come to my business and try to get me to buy a full-page ad in the Yellow Pages. Today, customers don't find businesses in the Yellow Pages. Who has a phone book anymore? Today, you need an online presence. That means having a good website and doing things such as search engine optimization (SEO) so that when customers search for keywords such as "moving company Atlanta," your moving company pops up on the first page of Google's organic search results. In the early days of the Internet, people would find businesses using desktop computers or laptops. Today, people use their smartphones. As a business owner, that means having mobile apps and responsive websites that can automatically adjust the viewing experience whether someone is visiting your site using a smartphone, tablet, desktop, or even TV.

Marketing is fluid. What worked in the past won't necessarily work in the future. How are your customers changing? How are they perceiving your business? Is your business changing depending on how your customers behave?

Smart Marketing Framework

I want to give you a framework to improve your marketing. It's called the Smart Marketing Framework, and it has five components:

In our online mastery courses and live seminars, we help you master the art of marketing. You see, it's not enough to just read about marketing and say, "Oh! That's a good idea!" Reading about something and being able to do it well are two different things. It's like the difference between reading about how to play the piano and actually playing the piano well. In our online courses, live seminars, and advanced mastermind groups, we help you become a master of marketing.

For now, let me describe the basics of the Smart Marketing Framework. The first component is customer experience. That means laying out your customers' experience from start to finish. What triggers the thought, *I need this problem fixed?* How do your customers search for solution providers? What makes you stand out among the solution providers? It could be as simple as being the most convenient one. For instance, when I called a plumbing company to fix my garbage disposal, the technician put a sticker with the company name and phone number on my garbage disposal. If the garbage disposal ever breaks again, the company's phone number is right there for me to call. Or maybe your company stands out among the solution providers because you have implemented reputation-management strategies to optimize positive reviews online. How is the customers' experience when they first contact you? How is the customers' experience when they are getting the service or buying the product? I remember going to a sushi restaurant that takes only cash. I spent almost sixty dollars on the meal only to realize that I might not have that much cash on me. Why would you ever make it difficult for your customers to pay you? By trying to save 2 or 3 percent in credit-card-transaction fees, the business ended up losing a customer altogether. How is the customers' experience after they leave? How can you make the entire customer experience smoother from start to finish?

The second component of the Smart Marketing Framework is to encourage repeat purchase. What can you do to encourage repeat purchase? Perhaps it's implementing some kind of reward program or loyalty program that rewards customers for doing business with you again in the future. I want you to make it easy for your customers to do business with you. For instance, you could give your customers a stamp card on which they collect ten stamps and get the next item free. But how many people will remember to carry your stamp card with them? Maybe people can use their phone number or e-mail to track their rewards and view the rewards directly on their smartphones.

The third component is to encourage referrals. Can you design a referral program and systemize it? Maybe every time people leave a good review, they automatically receive a special thank-you from you along with a special discount to come back again and a special discount for their friends and family. Maybe you e-mail your existing customer database every six months asking for referrals. Maybe your customers can work their way up the ladder (for example, Bronze VIP, Silver VIP, Gold VIP) to receive special benefits at your business, and the way to move up the ladder is either to do a certain amount of repeat business or to provide referrals.

The fourth component is to encourage larger purchases. Right after your customers decide to buy something, you may ask them if they want to upgrade their order or buy something related that complements their order. Another strategy to encourage larger purchases is to build trust through free stuff before you ask for the sale. For instance, I was advising a financial planner charging $300 for a one-day seminar who was having trouble filling the room. Having to spend an entire day with someone you don't know and paying $300 for it are commitments that are too big for new customers. Instead, I recommended that the financial planner give free two-hour evening seminars. *Free* is a good price, and two hours is less of a time commitment than spending a whole day. The purpose of the free two-hour seminar was to build trust. At the end of the evening seminar, the financial planner would promote his one-day seminar. I told him that he could charge a higher price for the exact same one-day seminar because new customers have already spent two hours listening to him and now trust him as an expert. He charged $997 for the one-day seminar and filled the room.

The fifth component of the Smart Marketing Framework is to obtain better feedback from your customers. Things are constantly changing, and you need good feedback to know how to improve. What can you do to obtain better feedback from your customers? For a property-management business, for example, there are four critical times to obtain feedback from renters. The first is when a prospective resident decides not to rent. Why did he or she choose to rent somewhere else? The second is when the residents just moved in. Are they totally happy with the move-in experience, or are they unhappy with the apartment? The third time is when the residents just made a maintenance request. Was the maintenance issue handled promptly and correctly? Was the maintenance staff courteous and professional? And the fourth time is when the resident's lease is going to expire in sixty days. Most good property managers will ask residents whether they want to renew their lease anywhere from forty-five to sixty days before their current lease is up. The time to survey residents on their satisfaction level is prior to asking about lease renewal so you can correct any issues before bringing up that topic. Having these four critical feedback points helps a property manager gauge the satisfaction level of renters and correct any issues right then and there. What are the critical feedback points at your business?

In summary, marketing is how customers perceive your business. Things like social media and advertising are just ways to affect the customers' perception of your business. There are many ways to improve customers' perception, and most of them don't cost much. To become a successful lifestyle business owner, you need to master the art of marketing. I call it an art rather than a science because marketing is fluid. Things are always changing, and what works in one area may not work in another area. Having said that, there are some general principles that can help you become a better marketer. The Smart Marketing Framework gives you five areas to work on that will improve your customer satisfaction and increase your revenues. Commit to mastering the art of marketing, and you will see the revenues of your company go up over time.

~ INVITATION TO ACT ~
What is your biggest takeaway from this chapter?

_____

_____

_____

_____

_____

_____

~ Free Training Videos ~
Visit www.LifestyleBusinessOwner.com
to download
your free training videos on
becoming a lifestyle business owner!

CHAPTER 9

Building a Great Team at Your Company

several years ago, I had a client named Thomas. Like many business buyers, Thomas is an ambitious person. He spent many years in the software industry and had several impressive accomplishments at the company he worked for. After years of being a corporate warrior, he decided to get into business for himself by buying a business. He wanted a business with an easily understandable operation so that anyone with good management skills could run it. After considering many potential business purchases, including a clothing store and a gas station, he ended up buying a garage-repair company.

Thomas did a lot of things right, but he made a critical mistake from the beginning. After he bought the business, he started making changes right away. From his perspective, he was a successful person who had accomplished a lot in the software industry and who believed his technology experience could bring the garage-repair industry into the twenty-first century. To the employees, however, he was just a new owner with no experience in garage repair telling everyone what to do and how to run things. One by one, the employees quit. Within the first few weeks of owning the business, Thomas had to deal with a massive turnover within the company. Needless to say, it was a very stressful and costly experience. He eventually recovered and filled all the vacant positions, but much of that stress could have been avoided if he had listened to my advice.

In all the years I've been selling businesses, I have found that it is actually very rare for the new owner to experience a massive employee turnover as Thomas did. Most of the time, the employees are more afraid of losing their jobs than you are of losing them. As long as you don't come in and start acting like you know more than everybody else does, the employees will learn to like you and trust you.

As a business buyer, you have just inherited a staff. Who should you keep, and who should you replace? At this point, it's too early to tell. My recommendation is to observe and learn the business for a while. If you come into the business too forcefully and start changing the way everything is run, the employees may quit, which will force you to fill vacant positions at an inconvenient time. If you observe, learn, and implement changes gradually, then the hope is that all of the employees will stay with you because they like you and they like the direction you are taking the company. If you eventually find that you have to replace someone, you will be doing it in your time frame instead of in the time frame being forced on you.

Effective employee management is crucial to your success as a lifestyle business owner. Some business owners do not like to have any employees because they think having employees means having headaches and stress. Unfortunately, not having any employees also means the business owner will be working all the time and will never be able to grow the business beyond his or her personal capabilities.

If you want to own a highly profitable business that gives you the amount of free time you desire and provides a sense of meaning and contribution, you need to learn how to build a great team. To help you master the art of employee management, I will share with you the Effective Employee Management Framework. There are five components to this framework: having the right mind-set, hiring well, training your employees well, retaining your employees well, and handling employee issues and challenges well. We will discuss each of these five components in detail.

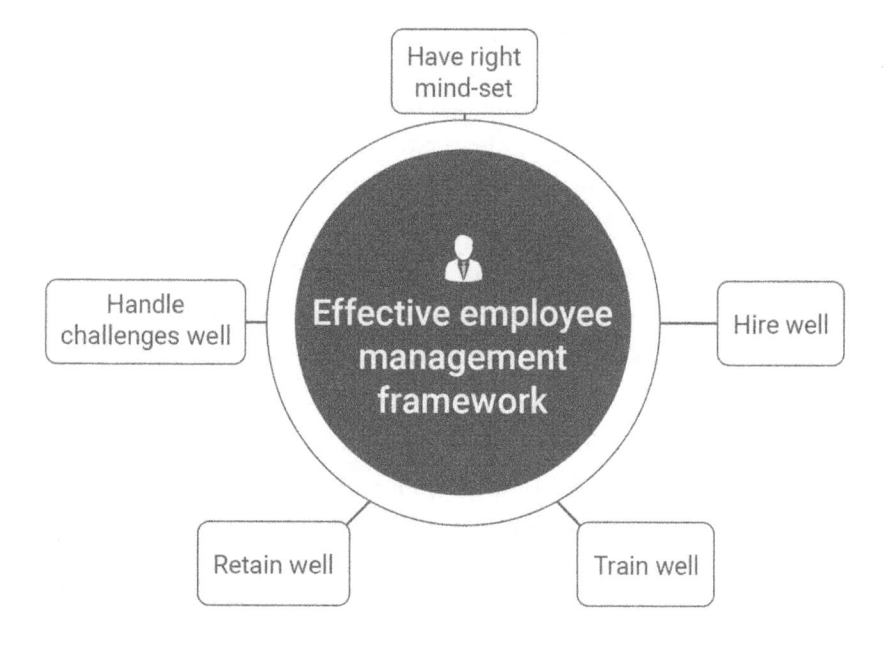

Component 1: Right Mind-Set

There is a mind-set very popular in the traditional business world that views the business as a giant machine. When the machine runs well, customers come into the machine at one end and profits come out the other end. Employees are viewed as replaceable parts of the machine. The role of the employees is to work in this giant machine and follow the rules. Creativity and individuality are not valued. What is valued instead is the employee's ability to follow procedures, not change anything, and work the machine the way it is designed to work. When the employee feels burned out and quits, you just hire someone else to step in and replace the employee.

Perhaps one of the best examples of a well-systemized machine is McDonald's. Have you ever noticed that McDonald's is usually run by high-school kids or low-wage employees without much education? Whether you like McDonald's as a business or not, you have to admire how well the McDonald's system runs. No matter who is working that day or where you are in the country, you can always count on getting the exact same burger, fries, and customer experience every time you walk into a McDonald's. The consistency of the McDonald's experience is one of the secrets to its profitability.

McDonald's is a well-oiled machine. It doesn't need to rely on a skilled chef to create great-tasting fries. In fact, the cooking operation is so automated that any high-school kid with minimal training can push a few buttons and make you some McDonald's fries. When a business is automated to the extreme, the employees are entirely replaceable. You can operate the business with mainly minimum-wage workers, and there are many people available to replace an employee if someone quits. In the traditional world of business, where profit is the only thing that matters, owning a McDonald's would be akin to owning the ultimate profit-making machine.

Unfortunately, this worldview of treating your business as a machine and seeing employees as replaceable parts has a number of unintended consequences. One, the practice is dehumanizing. You are no longer seeing your employees as human beings but are seeing them simply as replaceable parts in a machine. Whether your employees are happy with their jobs has little significance, because you can replace them easily. You can work them until they can't take it anymore, and then you can hire someone else who is willing to step in. The practice is not only dehumanizing to the employees but also dehumanizing to the owner. Perhaps more important than how much money you make is the answer to the question of what kind of person you are you becoming. To feel a deep sense of happiness and fulfillment in your business, you need to *like* the kind of person you are becoming.

Two, this mechanistic view of business robs your company of the potential for human ingenuity and creativity. Each person has so much to contribute to your business, but he or she gradually learns in an unspoken way that his or her ideas are not really valued because the business owner cares only about having a machine part that simply does the job it is supposed to do. Some of the most innovative companies actively encourage their employees to work together and find ways to improve the company's operations. Yes, the employees are working in the business, but they are also helping the owner work on the business. The employees are given the opportunity to improve their work environment and voice ideas about how the business could be better run. When you foster a work environment that people want to work in, they will be intrinsically motivated. No number of bonuses, incentive programs, or performance reviews can spark the twinkle in your employees' eyes as when they feel fired up to work for you.

Many large corporations end up treating their employees like replaceable parts in a giant machine. As a small business, you may not be able to offer the same level of benefits and compensation a large corporation can afford to offer. In order to attract good employees, show your people that you really care. Good employees want to feel like they are valued. They want the human connection. When you value your people as human beings and treat them well, they will feel alive. Customers will see this and choose to do business with you over doing business with a big corporation.

Rather than seeing their business as a machine and employees as parts in the machine, lifestyle business owners see their business as a living organism and employees as crucial parts of the organism. In a machine, every part is dead. In a living organism, every cell is alive. You intuitively know to treat something dead and something alive very differently. When something is alive, you need to foster and nurture it. You need to pay attention to its environment. You need to let it rest instead of working it to death.

Caring about your employees as human beings is essential to your success as a lifestyle business owner, but it does not mean you get to make bad business decisions. If an employee wants a raise but the business does not have the money, giving your employee the raise anyway will put not only your business in danger but also the livelihood of your employees if you go out of business as a result. When lifestyle business owners are faced with a tough choice between making a good business decision and caring about an employee, they do their best to think outside the box and brainstorm how they can do both. In the example above, I may put the challenge back in the hands of the employee and say, "Steve, I want you to make the most amount of money possible in my company. Given where we are right now, I can't give you a raise. However, if you can help me grow the business, we can come up with some goals together to increase your pay. Sounds good?"

You need to care about your business as much as you care about your employees. Are you the warm business owner who is your employees' best friend and lets your employees have whatever they want, or are you the cold business owner who puts business first and treats employees as replaceable parts? The truth is that neither extreme is healthy. Lifestyle business owners walk a fine line between the two; they find ways to make good business decisions and treat their people well.

If you are a parent, think about how you might guide your teenagers. You care about them a lot, but sometimes you need to show some tough love. You don't want to micromanage them, but you also don't want to let them have totally free reign. You see things they don't, but they also see things you don't. You give them opportunities to carry on without you, and you are there to support them when they fall. Being a parent of teenagers is not easy. It requires you to bring out your best self rather than succumbing to your lower self. Being a good boss is no different. You need to be at your very best, because your employees deserve your very best.

Following are the attitudes that lifestyle business owners should adopt when it comes to their employees.

- The owner cares deeply about the well-being of each employee but is not held hostage by any key employee, because the business is set up so that even if the most "irreplaceable" employee leaves, it will continue to survive.
- Instead of using military-style leadership, in which the owner gives orders and expects everyone to obey without question, the owner fosters an environment in which people are jazzed to come to work. These owners ask their employees, "What kind of work environment would make you feel jazzed to come to work every day, and how can we be more like that?"
- The owner understands that what is not said is often more powerful than what is said. If the owner says, "I value your input," but acts otherwise, the employees will soon pick up on the unspoken message and stop questioning authority for fear of losing their jobs. Every company has a set of written, spoken rules and a set of unwritten, unspoken rules. The owner's actions speak much louder than his or her words. To make any

kind of meaningful change, it is the unwritten, unspoken rules that need to be addressed.

Component 2: Hire Well

If you create an awesome work environment in which people want to work, your good employees will want to stay. If there is a job opening, candidates will be clamoring to apply, because people talk. If you've ever complained about a terrible job or told your friends how happy you are with your job, you know that word gets around. When you foster a work environment people want to be a part of, your good employees will probably tell their friends to apply.

Finding good employees is easy when you create an awesome work environment, because that's where the good employees want to work. If your current company experiences constant employee turnover, no amount of "how to hire good employees" training can prevent the good employees you've hired from quitting. Without turning the vicious cycle around, you will only experience more people quitting, more open positions to fill, fewer good candidates applying (because word gets around), more new employees who are not fully trained, and a demoralizing work environment, which leads to more people quitting and the cycle repeating again. If your company has high employee turnover, you need to take a hard look at whether your company's culture, unspoken rules, and work environment are toxic.

Even in the best companies, there will be times when someone is leaving and a vacant position needs to be filled or when the company is growing and a new position has been created. How do you go about finding the best talent for the position?

Believe it or not, the best talents are not cheap. No one is stupid. If John is a highly qualified employee who is able to get job offers paying $80,000 a year, he is probably not going to accept a position that pays much lower. As a business owner, you need to understand that there is a minimum salary the best talent will work for. We call this magic number the market rate, and it is different for every position, industry, and geographic location.

Your goal is to attract the best talent without paying too much, not to attract mediocre talent because you want to save money. If you don't pay at least the market rate, the best talent won't come. If you are not sure what the market rate is, it is better to err on the side of paying too much so you at least hit the minimum. Usually, the more you pay someone, the longer that person will stick around.

If you find a top talent but are hesitant to offer pay on the very high side, one possibility is to set up an incentive pay situation. The person gets a fair base salary and incentive pay based on performance. If the person performs well, he or she gets compensated at a level far greater than the typical top pay for the position.

How do you find the market rate of the position you are looking to fill? There are several ways. Talk to business owners in your industry. Look at what your competitors are paying. Ask the seller you just bought the business from. Look at your own experience. An excellent resource is GlassDoor.com, a website where employees voluntarily disclose how much their job position gets paid at their company.

Now that we've talked about how much pay you should offer, let's talk about the actual hiring process. The biggest mistake I see small-business owners make when it comes to the hiring process is basing the hiring decision on the interview. You can rule out the worst candidates from the interview, but it is often difficult to tell the difference between an average candidate and a top-notch candidate from the interview alone.

Much research has been done on the subject of interviews, and the findings show that the interview is only about 15 percent accurate at predicting job performance. That means 85 percent of the time, the job interview tells you nothing.

There are a number of reasons that explain why the job interview is such a poor predictor of job performance. One, your judgment is affected by the order of the interviews. If you interview five candidates, you will tend to remember the first and last candidates most because they make a lasting impression on your memory. Two, your judgment tends to get affected by impression management. Some candidates are better than others at controlling the impressions people have of them. If a candidate compliments you, you will tend to like him or her better. Third, your judgment tends to be affected by people who share common things with you. If you and the candidate both come from the same town, went to the same school, or share the same hobby, you will tend to like the candidate better. Four, the sad truth is that people tend to hire physically attractive people over unattractive ones, even though it has nothing to do with the job description. Finally, some candidates will exaggerate and lie during the interview, making them sound like the most amazing candidates—until you find out otherwise after they have been hired.

Rather than making the interview the first step of your hiring process, I recommend making the interview your last step. Since the interview is only 15 percent accurate at predicting job performance, your hiring decision should be mostly made prior to the interview. The interview should be used only as a confirming indicator, helping you confirm that your hiring choice is in fact the best one.

So how do you make the bulk of your hiring decision without relying on the interview? There are a few steps you should take before you ever schedule the interview. First, review the job application, cover letter, and résumé carefully. Ensure the qualifications for the job are met, and look for long gaps in employment, which may require further explanation. If attention to detail is a trait you are looking for, check for spelling mistakes. The cover letter can also give you clues as to how well the candidate writes.

Second, call the candidate's references before you conduct the interview. The most important reference to call is the candidate's former employer. Ideally, you want to speak with several former employers if the candidate has had several jobs prior to applying at your company. Be specific with your questions. Good questions to ask include "What are three positive things about this person?" and "What are three negative things about this person?" as well as "Would you hire this person again?"

Third, administer tests and simulations that allow you to see how the candidate actually performs the job duties. This is the closest we can get to predicting job performance short of hiring the candidate and seeing how he or she does on the job for a day. In other words, think about the job duties and devise a test to assess the candidate's ability to perform those duties. If you need someone to be good at Excel, find or create an Excel test. If you are hiring a maintenance technician, test the candidates on their maintenance knowledge. A person's intelligence can predict job performance with 50 percent accuracy, which is way better than the 15 percent accuracy offered by job interviews. I recommend an intelligence test such as the Wonderlic Personnel Test, which is a fast and cost-effective way to gauge someone's intelligence. Larger organizations often administer "cultural fit" tests. For instance, the best-performing employees at various positions are asked to take a personality test, and the incoming candidates' personalities are compared against the personality profiles of the best-performing employees. I like to use the Myers-Briggs Type Indicator to better understand the strengths and weaknesses of the candidate. Do what makes sense for your company and budget. At the very least, conduct one or two tests on the applicants. An effective test does not have to be expensive.

If the candidate has passed your first three steps, you should already have a pretty good idea of who you want to hire. Invite the person in for an interview as a final confirming step. A structured interview is more accurate at predicting job performance than a chat is. A structured interview looks something like this: prepare a list of questions in advance, and ask each question one by one. As the candidate answers each question, rate each response on a scale from one to five. After the interview, add up the scores for each question to come up with the total score for the person. If the total score is above a certain number acceptable to you, the candidate passes the interview. Again, the interview should be pass/fail only because it is not a good tool to distinguish the best candidates from the average candidates. As long as the candidate did not fail the interview, the passing score is enough as a confirming step.

It is important for you to be as proactive and efficient as possible during the hiring process. If you spot a good candidate, don't wait two weeks before getting back to him or her. If you wait too long, the candidate may be hired by another company. This is especially true if you are in an industry where good talents are hard to come by. I know you have a lot of other things on your plate, but make time to hire well. Go through those résumés. Call the references. Administer your tests. Conduct structured interviews. And most importantly, jump on the opportunity to hire a great talent when you see one.

Component 3: Train Well

If your employees are not properly trained, you will have a hard time becoming hands-off. Once you've hired the best talent, you need to provide them with the tools and training to succeed. One of the best ways to train your employees is to train them from the employee-training manual, which is a manual that you will write. You will write a manual for each type of job. If you own a carpet-cleaning business, you will write a manual for the employees who sell jobs to the customers and a manual for the production labor. If you own a restaurant, you will write a manual for the waitstaff and a manual for the kitchen workers. If you have a manager, you will write a manual just for the manager on how to manage your business.

Perhaps you are not a good writer. Don't worry. This is not about writing an award-winning novel. It's about teaching your employees how to do their jobs. As long as the directions are clear, you have done your job. So what should your employee-training manual contain?

1. *Cover page.* I believe in being professional. The cover page should have your company logo and the title of the training manual. If you are writing a training manual for the receptionist, the title would be *Receptionist Training Manual.*

2. *Table of contents.* A training manual can get pretty lengthy. Make it easy for people to read through yours and find certain information by providing a table of contents. As the author of the training manual, you will create the table of contents after you've written all the other sections.

3. *Welcome letter.* Start out by being positive. Welcome the new employee to your company and show appreciation that he or she has decided to come on board. If you have existing employees and are implementing the employee-training manual for the first time, use the welcome letter as an opportunity to thank them for being part of the team and explain your intentions. A great way to explain your intentions is to state what you do not intend and contrast it with what you do intend. For instance, you could write, "If you are wondering why I am putting everything into a formal training manual, please allow me to explain. I am not

trying to micromanage you or dictate how you should do your job. I value you as a person very much and would love to get your input on how we can make our work environment better for everyone who works here. My intention for developing this training manual was to formally document our company policies and describe the most effective way to perform certain tasks. If you have a better way to get something done than the method described in this training manual, please let me know and I would be more than happy to update the manual. You are an integral part of what makes this company work, and I want you to be happy working here. I am excited to help bring our company sales and employee satisfaction to the next level and would love your help and input in making this happen."

4. *Company background.* What is the history of the company? What does the company stand for? What makes your company different from your competitors? What are some of the challenges facing the company today? What must the company get right if it is to succeed as a company? It is really important for your employees to understand why they are working at this business and why what they do matters. Sure, people work because they need money to pay the bills, but your business can be so much more than just a paycheck-dispensing machine. People want to be part of a winning team. People want to be part of something that matters. People want to be proud of where they work. Even if your business is as mundane as a gas station, remind your team why your business matters. Maybe for the last thirty years, this gas station has been providing the fuel and food people need to get to where they are going—whether it's getting to work, getting home, or going somewhere fun. Maybe the company is about treating everyone who comes in with a smile, so employees have the chance to brighten at least one hundred people's days every day. Maybe people who work here have always prided themselves in maintaining a spotless facility so visitors and locals alike feel welcome in this part of town. What's your company about? Where was the company in the past, where is it today, and where is it going?

5. *Exactly how employees are paid.* People want to know exactly how they will be paid. Are you paying them by check or automatic deposit? Are you paying them hourly, a fixed salary, commission only, or a combination? How often are you paying them? Can they earn bonuses? How do they move up if they apply themselves? How often do you review their performance with them to see if a pay raise or pay cut is necessary?

6. *Company policies.* These are the rules that every employee must follow. They include what time they are supposed to come to work, when they can take a lunch break, how many sick days and vacation days they can take, what the computer policy is, what expenses you pay for versus what expenses the employees pay for, how much insurance you provide, what kinds of decisions they are allowed to make, and so on. All your policies should be spelled out here. If your employees cannot disclose company secrets, spell them out in this section. This is what you will hold your employees accountable to. If they break a company policy, the penalties should be clearly spelled out. There should be no question as to what you expect of them.

7. *Job description.* Give them an overview of their job. What does their job entail? What are their job duties? What activities should they do every day? What activities should they do once a week? What activities should they do once a month? Once a quarter? Once a year? What should they already know how to do without you having to train them (the minimum qualifications)? What should they know about this job (the pros and cons)?

8. *Step-by-step directions for how to do their job.* Most business owners keep this information in their heads and try to train employees orally. Unfortunately, most people forget what they hear. For your training to be effective, you need to write out step-by-step directions for how their job should be performed. If the job relies on using a special computer software, you might include screenshots and step-by-step directions for what buttons to click. If the job involves filling out forms, you want to write down step-by-step exactly how to fill out each form. Remember, you only have to write all this down once. Once you've done it, you can

train all future employees exactly the same way. In fact, you can even pass the training manual on to your manager, and he or she will be able to train all future employees exactly the same way you do. This is the key to systemizing a business.

9. *How their job serves the overall mission of the company.* Do you know why so many employees are unmotivated? Because they do not feel that what they do is meaningful. If you hire someone to make cold calls all day, that employee may begin to feel depressed or bored pretty soon. You need to describe how the cold-calling efforts are helping the company grow. You need to help the employee see how important his or her job is to the success of the company. If you are hiring a janitor, you need to explain how the janitor's work is affecting the customers' perception of the company. If your employees understand why they are important and how they fit into the overall picture, they will begin to see that their jobs are not just repetitive, meaningless tasks. They are actually contributing to something greater.

10. *Contact information.* Here you include the contact information of anyone your employees might need to reach. This could include your cell phone number, the manager's cell phone number, your suppliers' phone numbers, the bookkeeper's phone number, the computer technician's phone number, even the phone numbers of nearby pizza take-out places. Again, your employees need to know who to call for different kinds of situations.

11. *Important passwords.* Many businesses today have a lot of computer passwords that are hard to keep track of. If this is the case for your business, provide a list of log-in credentials your employees will need. Alternatively, use a password manager that keeps track of all the individual passwords, and the employees gain access only to one central password. The employees can't see the individual passwords to each site—they only know the central password. Each employee's central password is different depending on which individual sites they need access to. If the employee gets terminated, you just disable his or her central password.

12. *Terms employees should be familiar with.* There are certain terms and jargon that only the people in your line of business would know. For instance, every mortgage broker knows what an ARM is. But if a new receptionist is hired, he or she might have no idea what you are talking about. It's worth your time to step back and think about all the jargon you use that the new employee might not be familiar with. Provide employees with a list of terms and invite them to ask you questions if they don't understand something.

13. *Recommended tools.* For certain jobs, there might be expenses that employees are responsible for that are highly recommended because they can increase effectiveness. For instance, if you are hiring a salesperson, you might recommend having a smartphone or fast laptop so he or she can be more effective.

14. *Statement that the employee has received, understood, and agreed to comply with the information contained in the training manual.* This is a statement that the employee will need to sign and give you a copy of. If there is ever a question or dispute, you can use the employee's signature to keep him or her accountable. Also, you should include a sentence stating that the training manual is company property and that the employee cannot make a copy or share the training manual with anyone else. If the employee ever leaves your company, he or she must return the training manual.

Writing these employee-training manuals can take some time, but it's time well spent. If there is ever a question about how a job is to be done, you can ask your employees to open up their training manuals. If your employees ever ask you about their vacation days or sick days, ask them to look it up in the company policies section. You need to hold your employees accountable to the training manual. If your employees ever deviate from your detailed directions, you should talk with them about it right away.

Employee training is a continual process, and the employee-training manual should be revised over time. If you or your employees discover a more effective method of doing something, the step-by-step directions should be revised so that your employees can utilize the more effective method from then on. The best companies set aside funds in the budget to train their employees and help them become more effective. The employee-training manual provides a good start for new employees and provides consistency for existing employees. After the initial training, continue to help your employees improve by encouraging continuing education.

Component 4: Retain Well

It will be difficult for you to become a lifestyle business owner if you cannot retain good employees. There are three keys to pay attention to if you want to retain good employees.

Key 1: Good compensation package. At the end of the day, people need money to pay the bills, and good employees won't stay long if your compensation package is poor. This doesn't mean you have to offer the highest compensation in the industry, but bear in mind that it is hard to keep good employees if your compensation is below a certain level. I don't offer the best benefits in the industry, but I don't offer the worst. The benefits I offer are comparable to what my competitors offer, and the pay I offer is at least high enough to attract the best talent to work at my company. If it makes sense for the position, something I like to do is to give people a modest base salary with the incentive to make more if the company does well. Your employees are incentivized to make the business run well, and you are not burdened with a huge base salary if business is down. In other words, I am asking my employees to share the risks and rewards with me. If business is bad, their pay is lower than the pay they would have received if I had committed to a salary-only arrangement. If business is good, their pay is higher than with a salary-only arrangement. Now that my employees and I are on the same page, we all work hard to make business good.

Key 2: Healthy company culture. More important than offering the highest pay is offering a work environment that your employees feel jazzed about every day. Your employee-training manual spells out the spoken, written rules of the company, but your company culture is the unspoken, unwritten rules of the company. If the unspoken rule is that the person who works the longest hours gets rewarded, a good employee who values work-life balance may not stay for long. If an employee brings up a concern and is told she's too sensitive, she will quickly learn the unspoken rule that some topics are not allowed to be brought into the open. If left unchecked, the work environment can turn toxic quickly, which is a major cause of good employees quitting.

Key 3: Know what matters to each person. Part of caring about your employees is knowing what matters to each person. Some people love to be recognized in front of others, whereas others hate it. Some people value the ability to learn new things and start to lose motivation if their job duties become too repetitive. Some people value flexibility. If employees can work from home sometimes, not have set hours as long as they get the job done, have the ability to take extra unpaid days off, and so on, they may really appreciate the flexibility and stay with you for the long-term. Know what matters to each person. The more motivated your employees are, the less you will have to micromanage them.

If you attend any of our lifestyle business owner seminars, you will hear me stress again and again the importance of creating a great work environment. If the work environment is toxic, the best employees won't stay for long. So how do you provide a great work environment? I am going to share with you a very important principle. If you can apply this principle, your employees will feel like they are part of a team, they will be motivated, and they will feel like they are making a difference. It's a principle that sounds very simple, but many business owners do not follow it because they let their ego get in the way. If you are willing to learn, this principle will do wonders for you.

The principle is this: *involve your employees in the decision-making process.* As you move closer to becoming a lifestyle business owner, it's going to be your employees who are dealing with your customers on a day-to-day basis. You are not going to be there all the time, and your employees will have a better picture of what's going on than you do. If something goes wrong, your employees will often notice it before it gets to you.

So why not involve your employees in the decision-making process? If you are trying to design a new marketing piece, ask your employees about which marketing pieces have worked well in the past and what they think the new marketing piece should contain. If you are trying to improve your customer service, ask your employees to tell you what customers are saying about your service. I always share the company's financial statements with the store manager. I want my manager to know all the income and expenses of the company so he or she can make better decisions to increase profits.

Employees feel valued and feel like they are making a difference when you ask them for their input. If you are trying to redesign their job description, ask them how they would do it. Involving employees in the decision-making process works so well in motivating employees that it often works better than giving bonuses. Yes, you heard that right. Getting employees involved in making business decisions often works better than giving bonuses.

A great idea to implement is to get every employee involved in tracking sales. Your total sales number for the month is the biggest indication of your business growth. Get everyone excited to increase sales! Share with your employees your sales figures each month. Also share with them your target for the month. And if everyone works together to achieve the target, have some kind of celebration.

Are you getting the idea here? You are trying to involve your employees in your business as much as possible. Get them involved with increasing sales. Ask for their input on how you can make your business grow. Do you have to follow what they say? Not necessarily. All you are doing is getting them involved and asking them for their input. You are still free to make the final decision, but people get behind what they help create.

The principle of getting your employees involved extends beyond making business decisions. It can also apply to giving employee benefits. With health-insurance costs increasing each year, why not let your employees participate in the health insurance? I always let my employees participate in the insurance plan; the employees pay 25 to 50 percent of the costs. The idea is to educate your employees that there is no free lunch. If they want health insurance provided by the company, they need to contribute part of the cost. You are in business to thrive in a competitive environment, not to hand out free things to your employees. Large corporations can afford to hand out better benefits than you can, and that's okay. There are people who prefer to work for small businesses because there is often more freedom, flexibility, and genuine caring. These people understand the tradeoffs, so don't feel like you have to match the benefits offered by big corporations.

When you involve your employees in the business decision-making process, they will begin to learn that every action has a consequence. They can't just do whatever they want and expect pay raises. If they want pay raises, they have to work hard to increase sales, give you input on how to make things better, and provide excellent service to your customers. Getting your employees involved in making decisions gives them a clear direction to go in if they want pay raises. They'll begin to understand that pay raises don't just come out of thin air. If they want to get raises, they'll have to work hard as a team to increase sales for you. When you share your company's financial statements with your manager, he or she will have to carefully control the expenses to make sure that the expenses do not get out of hand.

Component 5: Handle Challenges Well

Even in the best companies, the business owner will encounter employee issues and challenges. How you handle employee concerns, conflicts, and problems can either contribute to a healthy company culture or set it back. Remember, the unspoken and unwritten rules of your workplace are much more powerful than the written ones. It is important to have the written rules as suggested in the employee-training manual, because documentation is key to systemizing your business and making it run well without you someday. But it is the unspoken and unwritten rules that will dictate how well your written rules are followed.

I once encountered a company in which there was a great mismatch between the written values and the unwritten values. The company had beautiful brochures touting its values, such as collaboration and putting people first. In practice, however, there was little of either. It was very much a top-down, command-and-control, obey-or-get-fired culture, and the employees quickly learned not to voice any opinion contrary to what the boss said. If there was a problem, you kept your mouth shut. Voicing something controversial was the equivalent of kissing your promotion (or job) good-bye. At this company, it didn't matter that the CEO said the company valued collaboration. The employees knew what was truly valued and followed the unwritten rules instead.

The reason I am bringing up the difference between the written and unwritten rules is that every employee challenge is an opportunity for you to show whether you really mean what you say. If you say you expect your employees to come to work on time but you don't confront them when they are five minutes late, they will learn the unwritten rule that being five minutes late to work is okay. If you write in your policy manual that the company does not tolerate sexual harassment but you make gender-based jokes at the workplace, your employees will learn the unspoken rule that a sexual-harassment-free workplace isn't really valued. If you say you value feedback from your employees but completely lash out or shut down when an employee brings up some controversial feedback, people will learn that it's not okay to disagree with the boss even when they see something that may not be in the company's best interest.

Your ability to handle tough conversations well will greatly influence the level of toxicity at your company's workplace. If you can handle tough conversations well, people will appreciate what you do and feel safe to be who they are at your company. If you do not handle sensitive situations well, people will pick up the cues and behave the way you want them to in order to keep their jobs. They will slowly lose their liveliness within, however. Trust me. The best employees who can get jobs elsewhere will quit if the work environment is toxic.

So how do you handle employee issues and tough conversations well? First, don't avoid the issue. Avoidance of tough topics leads to undesirable side effects. Second, do it sensitively and don't lash out in verbal violence. Have a verbal conversation with the employee in private. Don't publicly criticize an employee, because you don't want to embarrass the employee in front of others. State what you saw, and state your feedback constructively. For instance, you might say, "I noticed that this is the second time you have been late to work this week. I understand that sometimes there are things outside of your control that cause you to be late. I want you to succeed at this company, and being here on time is important to making that happen. I am not saying I am unhappy with your performance. Other than this one issue, I am actually quite happy with your work. I just want you to know that punctuality is important at this company, because other people are counting on you. Will you make an effort to be here on time in the future?"

Whether the conversation is about being late, spending time on one's personal Facebook account at work, being sloppy and not following through, or any other of a variety of employee problems, the process is the same. Don't address the problem in public. Have a conversation with that employee in private, and do it calmly and constructively. I recommend having the conversation right after the incident instead of waiting. It could be as simple as, "Oliver, could you come here for a minute?" Then I close the door and have a private conversation with him. If the same issue happens again and again in different ways, the conversation is no longer about the issue but about the pattern. If verbal conversations don't fix the issue, you need to proceed to a written warning. If the written warning still doesn't fix the issue, you will need to proceed to firing the employee. Although I don't like to fire people for minor offenses, too many minor offenses lead to a mediocre employee. In *Good to Great,* Jim Collins says that good is the enemy of great. In other words, it's easy to let someone go if he or she is a terrible employee. It is a lot harder to let someone go if he or she is simply mediocre. If you settle for mediocre employees, though, your company will eventually become mediocre. I want great employees working at my company. Part of achieving greatness is not settling for mediocrity and letting mediocre employees go if I have to.

When firing an employee, some business owners might be tempted to just hand that employee a letter and walk away so they don't have to listen to the employee's sob story. Don't do that! You don't want angry employees leaving your company without having the chance to express how they feel. They can become hostile and cause problems in the future if you just hand them a letter and walk away. People's hostility and frustration go way down if you simply give them the opportunity to express how they feel. Bring them into your office and verbally let them know the reason you have decided to let them go. Be firm, direct, and honest about the termination. Let them know that the decision is final and that there is no room to negotiate the possibility of keeping them. If they start to argue with you, just listen to them and gently let them know that you understand how they feel, but the decision is final.

Before entering into the "you're fired" conversation, it helps to do some quiet reflection. What do you really want for yourself? What do you really want for this employee? What do you really want for the relationship? I don't like to end things on a bad note because I never know what the future may bring. Things can change in the future, and I may end up hiring this person back in a different capacity. If I am calm and professional during the firing process, this person may have increased respect for me and may end up spreading the word. What's more, a disgruntled former employee can cause problems, including lawsuits. To prevent things from ending on a bad note, make sure the termination doesn't come as a surprise. If something is not working, have a verbal conversation. If it's not fixed, proceed to a written warning. The termination conversation should happen only after the employee has received a written warning. Finally, in most cases you should have a replacement ready before you fire someone. Otherwise, you may be short-staffed and pressured to hire someone fast instead of taking your time to find the best candidate possible.

In summary, there are five areas to master in effective employee management: having the right mind-set, hiring well, training well, retaining well, and handling employee challenges well. If you master these five skills, you will have the confidence to build a great team at your company.

~ INVITATION TO ACT ~
What is your biggest takeaway from this chapter?

_____

_____

_____

_____

_____

~ Free Training Videos ~
Visit www.LifestyleBusinessOwner.com
to download
your free training videos on
becoming a lifestyle business owner!

CHAPTER 10

Making Your Operations Run Smoothly

We have now covered smart marketing and effective employee management. The next area you need to master in the journey of growing your business is making your business operations run smoothly. And what exactly does that mean? Well, have you ever been to a restaurant where the food was great one time but not so much the next time? Or the service was great one time but not so much the next time? In order to create the best customer experience, you must meet your promises consistently. And how do you meet your promises every single time no matter how busy you are or which employee is working that day? The operations component of your business must be working properly. The goal of operations is to deliver on your promises consistently, systematically, and automatically.

There are six components in the Smooth Operations Framework:

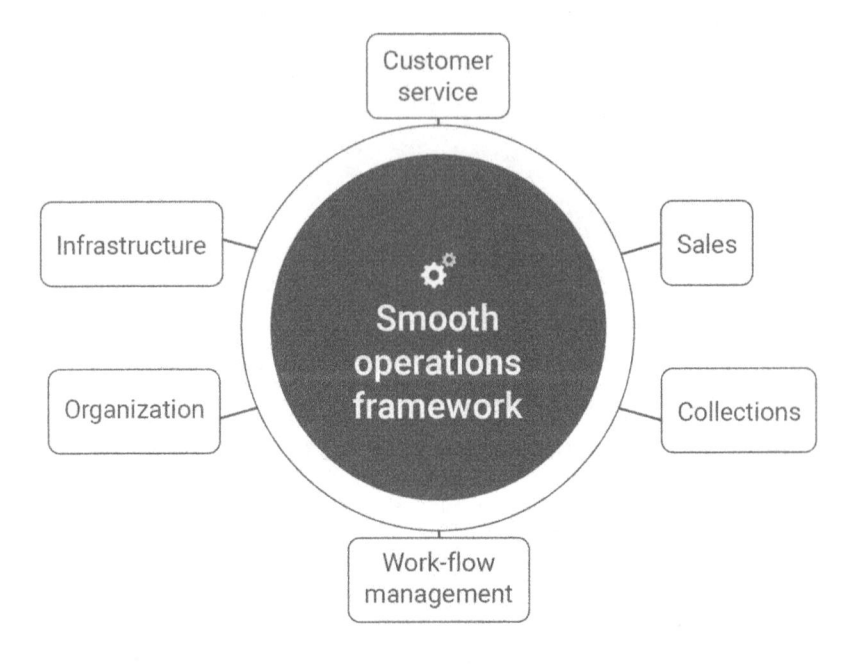

Let me briefly describe the six components, and then we will dive into each of them in detail.

- Customer service is how well you and your employees respond to your customers' needs.
- Sales is the persuasion process that makes people buy from you.
- Collections is making sure your customers pay you on time.
- Work-flow management involves creating a smooth process from the time the customer arrives to the time the customer leaves.
- Organization is about keeping good records so you know exactly how your business is doing at any moment in time.
- Having a good infrastructure means you have the necessary physical equipment as well as legal protection for your business to function at its best.

As you can see, working on operations may not be the most exciting task, but it is absolutely necessary if you want to become a lifestyle business owner. So let's go through these six components one at a time.

Component 1: Customer Service

Offering great customer service is crucial to the success of your business. With more and more customers looking at online reviews before calling a business, your online reputation can greatly affect how much business you get. Everyone who works at your company should be trained to provide excellent customer service. If a customer is not happy, work with the customer to reach a happy resolution. Rather than giving the customer's money back, I prefer to perform the service again or correct the situation for free. The rationale is that you want to send a message that your business is able to meet its promises. Giving people their money back almost sends the wrong message, which is that you can't do the job right. Obviously, there are exceptions to this rule. But everything must be done to protect the reputation of your business.

Too many business owners focus too much on the price and not enough on customer service. Here's what I believe: if your customer service is good enough, people will pay the price. Forget about discounting prices for mediocre service. Offer the best customer service and charge premium prices for it. Following are the five keys to offering excellent customer service.

Friendliness. Are your employees friendly to the customers? How friendly and professional is your showroom, lobby, or waiting area? Is it cluttered? What's the temperature in the room? Do you play background music? If so, what kind of music do you play and how loud is it? You have to pay attention to every little detail. There are many ways to be friendly, and the idea here is to create a welcoming and professional environment that goes beyond the expectations of your customers. You can even implement systems that will help your employees wow the customers. These could be simple things such as walking the customers to their car, attaching a mint with the receipt, remembering their names, sending them a birthday card, or encouraging your employees to perform one random act of kindness for one customer each day (and even setting aside business funds that allow your employees to do so).

Good communication. Employees who interface with customers regularly need to communicate well with them. Sometimes this is a matter of training. But you should know that not everyone will be able to relate well with your customers. You need to hire the right people who can relate and communicate well.

Knowledge. Your employees need to be well trained so they are knowledgeable about your products and services, forms and computer systems, and procedures for how to answer the phone, handle dissatisfied customers, handle an emergency, and so on. The more knowledgeable your employees are, the more confident they will be and the more hands-off you can be.

Follow-through. Your customers need to know that your business meets its promises. If you own a web-design firm and you promised the customer that the website would be ready in three weeks, you need to deliver the finished website in three weeks. What systems can you put in place to ensure that the promises made to customers are kept?

Effective conflict resolution. Sooner or later, your employees will encounter an angry customer. Are your employees trained on what to do? The objective should be to reach a happy resolution. Your employees need to come across to the customer as helpful rather than unhelpful. An unhelpful response might sound like this: "Sorry, this is company policy. There is nothing I can do about it." A helpful response might sound more like this: "I am hearing that you are upset because of this. I want to work with you to come up with a resolution you are happy with. There are some places where my hands are tied, and some places where we have flexibility. What does a happy resolution look like to you?"

Keep in mind that many people choose to shop at small businesses for the more personal feel. They don't want to be treated like a number in a database. Providing superior customer service is an edge that small businesses have over large corporations. Make your customer service shine, and you will attract a loyal following.

Component 2: Sales

In order for your business to survive, you have to make a sale. Selling a product or service to the customer is what brings in revenues. Without sales, your business won't survive. Essentially, there are three ways to increase revenues: bring in more customers, sell more to each customer, and sell to each customer more frequently. How can you do this effectively? How do you build so much trust that customers want to come back more often, buy more from you each time, and bring their friends and families to you?

The secret is to be an advisor, not a salesperson. Let me explain what I mean. Think about it. People are getting more skeptical these days. Consumers are becoming more sophisticated. A lot of the sales techniques that have worked in the past are no longer working. For example, have you ever heard a salesperson trying to make an appointment by saying something like this: "Mr. CEO, would you prefer to meet on Tuesday at ten o'clock or Wednesday at nine o'clock?" The sales technique here is giving people a choice between something and something rather than a choice between something and nothing. If the salesperson simply said, "Mr. CEO, would Tuesday at ten o'clock work for you?" the CEO could say either yes or no. Instead, the salesperson gave the CEO a choice between Tuesday and Wednesday, so the CEO is likely to pick one rather than saying no.

Well, the fact is that sales techniques like this are losing their effectiveness. If you use this technique on people, you will probably find that fewer and fewer people are influenced by it. Consumers are wary of salespeople. They don't want to feel like they are being manipulated into buying something because the salesperson uses sales techniques on them. In order for you to be effective at selling, you have to switch your mind-set from selling something to the customers to advising them on the best decision to make.

What does it mean to be an advisor instead of a salesperson? As an example, I want you to think of the most manipulative salesperson you can come up with—perhaps a used-car salesman. When you walk onto the car lot, the used-car salesman will probably use all the sales techniques he knows on you until you buy the used car. When you ask him which car you should buy, he will tell you undoubtedly that it is the car he is trying to sell.

Now imagine you are discussing your corporate tax returns with your CPA. You want to legally minimize the taxes you pay, but you don't know how to go about it. You are seeking tax advice from your CPA. You ask questions such as, "Do you think this is a good idea? Should I do this? Should I do that? What do you think is the best way to go?" Your CPA is objective. He or she may agree with you on some issues and disagree with you on others. If your CPA thinks what you are doing is a bad idea, he or she will tell you.

In the two scenarios above, your CPA is acting as the advisor, and the used-car salesman is the salesperson. But it's not the profession that determines whether you are an advisor or a salesperson. It's your attitude. Is the CPA selling you something? Of course! He or she is selling you knowledge, time, and tax services. Is the used-car salesman selling you something? Yes! You see, both the CPA and the used-car salesman are salespeople, but they approach sales in very different ways.

The used-car salesman throws you a bunch of sales techniques; the CPA doesn't. The used-car salesman has only one message: "I am the right person for you, and you know it's true." The CPA, though, may say something like this: "I may or may not be the right tax advisor for you. I specialize in giving tax advice to business owners with a net worth of $5 million to $30 million. If this fits you, I am the right person for you. If not, you are better off finding another CPA."

It is very easy for people to tell whether you are a salesperson or an advisor. Again, it's not what you sell that determines whether you are a salesperson or an advisor; it's how you approach the process. At my business brokerage, my job is to sell businesses to potential buyers. If you ever sit in one of my meetings with potential buyers, you will notice that I don't convince the buyers to buy a business. In fact, I will often tell the buyers why they should not buy the business they want to buy.

Let's pause for a moment. You have a product to sell. You have a buyer who wants to buy it. Who in their right mind would convince a buyer not to buy their own product? An advisor would. This is something that a salesperson would never do. But advisors regularly convince their buyers not to buy their product if they feel that it's not the best decision for the buyers to make.

In other words, the less you try to "sell" people, the more they will trust you. You want to come across as someone who gives recommendations rather than as someone who gives a sales pitch. Remember, though, that you need to give recommendations that are in the best interests of your prospects. If your only recommendation is "buy my product," your recommendation has just become a sales pitch.

When I explain to certain prospects why the business they want to buy is not a good choice, I might lose an opportunity to make that particular sale, but I have just gained a lot of credibility. The next question many prospects ask me is, "Well, if this is not a good business for me, do you know of any that would be good?" If I have a good business, I will show it to the prospect. If I don't, I will simply say, "Well, I don't have any good businesses that would fit you right now. When I see one, I will let you know."

And guess what? I now have a waiting list of prospects awaiting my phone call. When I see a good business that would fit one of them, I simply call that prospect up and say, "I think I have just found the right business for you." What do you think goes on in the mind of the prospect? Am I giving a sales pitch? No! The prospect knows that I am giving an expert recommendation. The prospect knows that I am not someone who would recommend just any business. If I think a business is good, it must be good.

In summary, forget about the sales techniques. People want an honest advisor they can trust, not a manipulative salesperson who knows all the different ways to close the sale. To be an advisor, you need to come across as an expert. In other words, you need to know your stuff. Explain the rationale behind your recommendations, and your prospects will appreciate your expert advice as well as your having their best interests in mind. From now on, give recommendations, not sales pitches. When you begin to act as an advisor instead of a salesperson, your prospects will trust you a lot more, and your effectiveness at sales will go way up.

Should the business owner personally be good at sales? That's a very good question. Many successful entrepreneurs have a background in sales and marketing, because you need a salesperson to bring in business. When entrepreneurs need to borrow money, you need good salesmanship to convince the banker to lend you money. Without a good salesperson in the company, your company won't last very long.

This leads to the question, what if you are not very good at sales? Here's my take on the subject. It is important for a business to have at least one good salesperson, but this person does not have to be the owner. It certainly helps if the owner is good at sales, but in the case that the owner isn't, it is not the end of the world.

If you are not personally good at sales, you just need to make sure that you have someone good on your team. One way to do this is to partner with a good salesperson. For instance, it is very common to see businesses that are owned by two people—one person is in charge of the sales and marketing, and the other person does all the background stuff.

If you are going to be the sole owner of the business and you are not very good at sales, you'll have to somewhat depend on hiring a good salesperson to bring in business. Unfortunately, good salespeople are hard to find. Hiring good salespeople involves a lot of trial and error. All the rules of interviewing and hiring employees still apply, and you want someone who is solid instead of someone who thinks he or she is a hotshot.

So where do you find good salespeople? Very often, you will find them from your competitors. Or you can find the top salespeople from other industries and train them in your industry. Depending on the nature of your business, your salespeople may or may not work five days a week from nine to five. It is not a good idea to pay your salespeople on salary only, because you want their pay to be somewhat performance-based. You should pay them on commission only or a combination of salary and commission.

When it comes down to it, whether you need to be personally good at sales depends on your job position. If you enjoy selling and you occupy a sales position, it is very important for you to be good at sales. If you don't enjoy selling and you would rather do more background work, there are ways around it. What's important is that the person doing the selling is good at sales.

Component 3: Collections

Making all the sales in the world won't do you any good if your customers don't pay you. For your business operations to run smoothly, you must be paid promptly by your customers. Depending on the industry, customers will have different expectations of when it is acceptable to pay you. In the restaurant industry, the customers are trained to pay you at the time of service. You provide the food, and the customers pay you right away. In the legal industry, the customers are trained to provide payment before the attorney has done any work. It is common for attorneys to collect thousands of dollars as a deposit (known as a retainer) before any work has been done. In the pressure-washing industry, it is common for the pressure-washing work to be done, an invoice to be sent, and the customer to pay thirty or forty-five days after the invoice is sent.

If your company sounds like the last example, in which the customers are given thirty to forty-five days to pay you after you've already delivered the product or service, all efforts must be made to attempt to receive payment sooner. If your sales are $750,000 per year, you can divide it by 365 days to get an average of $2,054.79 per day. If you are able to receive payment from your customers seven days faster, you could potentially gain an additional $14,383.56 in cash in your bank account (calculated by multiplying $2,054.79 by 7 days).

Here are six tips that will help you receive payment from your customers sooner.

Send invoices right away. Many companies send invoices on the last day of the month. If a job is finished on the second of the month, they wait till the thirty-first to send an invoice to the customer. That's twenty-nine days of not getting paid caused by your own delay. Your company should be sending invoices every day. If a job is finished on the second of the month, an invoice should be sent to the customer that day. If the job is large, you may even consider sending several intermediate invoices so that you get paid along the way instead of waiting until the entire job is finished.

Send invoices electronically. If you send your invoices through the postal service, it adds several days of delay before the customer even receives your invoice, not to mention the possibility of the invoice getting lost in the mail. In today's business world, you should deliver your invoices electronically for immediate receipt.

Double-check who you are sending the invoice to. If you send your invoice to the customer's general e-mail address (such as info@XYZCompany.com), your invoice could be held up by the customer for several days until all the e-mails are sorted and the invoice is forwarded to the person in charge of making payments. Ideally, you want to send your invoice directly to the person who handles paying invoices. This may seem like a no-brainer, but you'd be surprised how often invoices are not sent to the right person.

Encourage electronic payment. If your customers mail you a physical check, it creates several days of delay for the postal service to deliver the check to you. If you run to the bank once a week to deposit checks, it could be another few days until the check gets deposited into your bank account. If the check amount is large, the bank might even put a hold on it and create another week of delay before the funds are available. In today's business world, you should encourage all your customers to pay you electronically so that the funds show up immediately in your bank account. Another great tool is having a check scanner at your business so your employees don't have to run to the bank all the time.

Call the customer as soon as the payment is late. Many companies wait until the end of the month to call whoever is late for that month. Again, if the invoice is late by the fifth of the month and you wait until the thirty-first to call, you just created twenty-six days of delay. A phone call should be made to the customer the day the invoice is late. You should put systems in place so that every day, the invoices that become late that day pop up along with the customer's contact information for your store manager, bookkeeper, or accounts receivable person. The phone call should be friendly, courteous, and professional. You should also set a reminder to pop up if payment still has not been received after a certain number of days, so your company can make a second and third phone call to the customer. If the customer is local, an effective, though time-consuming, collections method is to show up at the customer's doorstep. Any late-paying customers should be flagged in the system so that if they want to buy from you in the future, they have to pay cash right away. Working on collections takes time, but collecting what's due to your business is crucial to the cash flow of your business. If you need to hire someone just to work on collections, do it. I've found that it's actually cheaper to hire a collections person for, let's say, twelve dollars an hour than it is to not have your customers pay you on time.

Be stingy with the terms you offer. Whether you allow your customers thirty, sixty, or ninety days to pay you will vary with the industry and the size of the customer. There are some large corporate customers that have policies requiring their vendors give them ninety days to pay their bills. As a small business, you have to watch your cash-flow needs. Allowing your customers a long time to pay you is one way to land big accounts, but you have to decide whether your business has the financial ability to weather the period of not being paid for ninety days or longer. In general, I recommend staying on the stingy side compared to your competitors. You want to win customers based on providing excellent service and customer experience rather than on giving your customers a longer amount of time to pay you than your competitors would. For many of my coaching clients, I recommend requiring all first-time customers to pay immediately (cash on delivery). If the customer wants to open up an account and have the convenience of paying later, the customer needs to fill out a credit application and have his or her references checked. All invoices should say "Due upon receipt" instead of "Net 30," meaning payment is due immediately instead of in thirty days. I recommend giving the very best customers ten days to pay. Some companies also impose discounts if their customers pay early and penalties if their customers pay late, which can be effective strategies to encourage prompt payment.

Component 4: Work-Flow Management

Work-flow management means creating a smooth process from the time the customer arrives to the time the customer leaves. When the customer arrives at your door, he or she has a problem that needs to be solved. A series of steps must happen for you to solve this problem. When the problem is solved, the customer pays you and leaves.

Think about every step that must take place when you perform a service for your customers. These steps are called work flow. The goal of work-flow management is to manage these steps to make the process more efficient.

If you've never done this before, I want you to write down every step that takes place from the time the customer walks in your door to the time the customer leaves. If you own an auto-repair shop, the work flow might look something like this:

1. The customer walks in.
2. The service advisor stands up and says, "Hi, how can I help you?"

3. The service advisor hands a pen and a Preservice Check-In Sheet to the customer.
4. The customer fills it out.
5. The service advisor checks to make sure the sheet is filled out completely and then asks the customer when he or she needs the car back.
6. The service advisor puts down the time on the check-in sheet.
7. The service advisor inputs the check-in sheet into the computer and prints out a job ticket.
8. The service advisor determines which technician to hand the job to (based on agreed-upon criteria).
9. The job ticket is handed over to the technician's jobs box, and the service advisor tells the technician that a new job has just been put in.

And so on and so forth. You would keep writing every step until the time the customer picks up the vehicle. Now, several things could happen as you try to write down every step in extreme detail. It could be easy for you, or it could be hard for you. If it's easy for you, it means your business is probably well systemized. If it is hard for you, it means either that you don't understand your business processes very well or that everyone does things differently each time so that you can't write down every step in extreme detail.

If you are having trouble writing every step down in extreme detail, this is one of the areas you will need to work on. Once you have written down every step, you need to check for inefficiencies. Perhaps there are things that slow your process down. Perhaps there are duplications. Perhaps there are things you can do to improve the efficiency of the process. Then you need to observe your business and make sure that every employee follows the steps you have written every single time. You see, although it is important for you to write down all the steps, it is equally important that your employees follow those steps every single time in order for your business to be well systemized.

The following are a few examples that demonstrate effective and ineffective work-flow management.

There is a Vietnamese restaurant in town. Every time I go there, I am amazed by how efficient everyone is. The restaurant can be completely full, yet literally

I can walk in, be seated within five seconds, have my order taken within one minute, and receive my food five minutes later. How can they be so fast when the restaurant is full of people? I have been watching all the little things they do to increase their efficiency. Let me describe some of them to you:

- All the water is poured in advance. They don't have waiters that bring you an empty cup and pour the water in front of you. Pouring water is a waste of time. Instead, they have a counter with at least fifty cups that have already been poured. When you walk in, the waiter walks to you with a cup with water already in it.

- Every table has a tray with at least one hundred pairs of chopsticks, thirty spoons, all the sauces you need, and all the napkins you need. This way, the waiters don't have to waste time bringing you the utensils or giving you more napkins when you run out.

- All employees know the purpose of their business. They are not there to provide a fine-dining environment. They are there to provide delicious Asian food quickly. That's why they don't walk you to your seat when you walk in. When you walk in the door, a waiter in the back of the room will make eye contact with you and hold up two fingers if he sees a party of two. If you hold up two fingers in return, he will point you to a table and you will walk to the table yourself. By the time you are there, the waiter has already set two menus and two cups of water on the table. If he recognizes you, he will simply ask you what you want. You might say, "Number 32 and Number 27." And he walks away. This all happens within the first fifteen seconds you walk into the restaurant. If you are a first-time customer, the waiter will come back thirty seconds later and ask you if you have decided yet. Either way, your order is taken within the first minute you are in the restaurant.

- When the server brings you the food, he brings your check with it. You see, if you have to ask for the check after you finish eating, that's time wasted. The check doesn't come in a black folder with fortune cookies on it. It's simply a piece of paper stating the amount and the following words: "Please pay cashier up front when you are done. Thank you!"

- When you pay, they have a fast credit-card machine. You hand them your credit card and you are done signing within thirty seconds. By the time you look back at the table at which you just ate, it has already been cleaned and the next set of customers has already been seated there.

It's pretty amazing watching the workers at this restaurant. Everybody hustles. The servers walk fast, and the chefs cook fast. There is very little verbal communication. The servers don't ask you how your day is, and they don't give a whole welcome speech as you sit down at your table. They simply come, take your order, and go. That restaurant, by the way, makes several million dollars in revenues a year. It is always full, yet you can always get your food within five minutes.

A few blocks away, there is a teriyaki place that I went to for lunch one day. I was in a hurry, so I ordered some chicken teriyaki to go. Nothing fancy—it was just chicken teriyaki. The restaurant had three customers, and guess how long it took them to bring me the food? It took them twenty-five minutes. After I got my food and started to walk out the door, the owner started to apologize profusely because they had forgotten to put my salad in the box. What a great example of inefficient work-flow management.

You see, there are things you can do to make your work flow more efficient. The more efficient you are, the happier your customers will be. People don't like to wait. But you can't just tell your employees to work faster, because they will probably make more mistakes. Usually, it's not that your employees work slowly on purpose. It's that there is something wrong with the system itself that is causing everything to slow down.

If you want to increase the efficiency of your work flow, you must change something in the system itself. You must examine each step of your operations and ask yourself, "Why do our employees do step X before they do step Y? Is it because that's the way it has always been done? Is there a better way to do this? What if we do step Y before step X? What if we do step X differently? What if we eliminate step X all together?"

When you start to ask these questions, you will start to notice things that are slowing everybody down. Suppose you own an auto-repair shop and your employees are constantly wasting time trying to find the right key for your customer's car. How about designing a system in which all the keys are kept in the same place and clearly labeled, so that there is no question about which key belongs to which car?

When you look at your work flow, one thing to consider is how much verbal communication takes place among your employees versus how much written communication takes place. Having too much verbal communication wastes time, and having too much written communication also wastes time.

Using the auto-repair-shop example, let's say you offer a free car wash with every service (an example of offering good customer service). Your front-counter person constantly has to go to the back and ask the car-wash person whether a car has been washed, and the car-wash person constantly has to come to the front and ask whether any car needs washing. You see, there is too much verbal communication. To save some time, buy two plastic bins. Place one bin near the car-wash person. Label this bin "To Be Washed." Place the second bin on the front counter and label it "Washed." When the technicians finish fixing a car, they will simply place the job ticket in the "To Be Washed" bin. Once it's washed, the car-wash person will bring the job ticket to the front counter and place it in the "Washed" bin.

If customers ever ask whether their cars are ready for pickup, the front-counter person simply has to glance at the bins; they will know exactly whether a car is ready or not. If the job ticket is placed in the "To Be Washed" bin and there are two other job tickets ahead of it, the front-counter person will know that there are two other cars that need to be washed before this one. He can now tell the customer approximately how long it will take for the car to be washed.

Having the bin system eliminates the time wasted in verbal communication. Now let me give you an example of too much written communication. Suppose every employee has to fill out a long and complex form before passing the form to another employee. A lot of things are not needed on the form, and there might even be duplications on different forms. For instance, if one form asks for the address and another form also asks for the address, your employees will have to write down the address twice. Too many forms can slow down your work flow.

The point I am trying to make is that too much written communication slows you down, and so does too much verbal communication. You have to examine every step of your work flow and think about where time is being wasted. The more you can increase your efficiency, the more business you can handle, which will lead to more revenues and higher customer satisfaction.

Component 5: Organization

Some people tend to be more organized than others. If you are constantly wasting time trying to find a particular piece of paper, your organization needs improvement. Being organized is closely tied to your work-flow management. The less organized you are, the more time you waste in getting the job done. Being organized is also closely tied to your marketing. Imagine a customer walking into your front counter or office and seeing piles of paperwork and clutter everywhere. What kind of impression do you think it creates in the minds of your customers? How do you think your customers will perceive your business?

Now, suppose you sent out coupons, and your customers bring the coupons back and ask for a discount. You give them the discount and take the coupons from them, but you don't keep the coupons in the same place. At the end of the month, how are you going to track the results of your advertising? How are you going to track how many coupons were brought back and the revenues that you made as a direct result of this coupon campaign?

In other words, if you want to run a profitable business, you need a good organization system. Being organized affects your efficiency, your customers' perception of you, and your ability to spend money wisely on advertising. A great way to be organized is to store as much information as possible electronically. If everything has to be printed out, all the pieces of paper can pile up quickly, not to mention all the storage space they take up. If I get a physical piece of paper with information I want to keep, I scan it, name the file, put the file in the appropriate folder, and shred the piece of paper afterward. I like using a secured cloud-storage service to store my data because should my computer fail, all the electronic data is not lost.

When I talk at my seminars about the importance of being organized, someone invariably says, "But, Aaron, even though I have pieces of paper everywhere, I know exactly where everything is!" That's fine. Some people's brains function better with a clean desk. Some people's brains function better with a messy desk. Personally, I belong to the latter group. If my desk is too clean, my juices aren't flowing. It's okay if you are like me. If you prefer having a messy desk, just make sure your customers can't see it. Remember, part of marketing is how people perceive you. You don't want your customers walking into your business and seeing crazy piles of paper everywhere.

Being organized not only saves time and improves people's perception of your business but also helps you minimize your taxes. In order to take advantage of all the possible tax deductions available to you, you need to have great records to back them up. I understand that taxes is one of those topics that can seem very complex and confusing for many business owners. Some taxes are due monthly, some are due quarterly, and some are due annually. When your business makes above a certain level of sales, sometimes you will need to switch from paying taxes quarterly to paying taxes monthly. To make matters worse, there are all sorts of agencies that collect taxes from you, and the forms they send you are not exactly easy to understand.

I recommend doing the following three things to keep organized for taxes:

1. *Meet with your CPA.* Ask your CPA about all the city, county, state, and federal taxes that your business needs to pay and when the due dates are. Rules and regulations change all the time. A good CPA stays up-to-date and informs you of the changes.

2. *Meet with your bookkeeper.* Have your bookkeeper set up a system for you so you always pay your taxes on time. Remember, the goal is to set up systems so you don't even have to think about it. Your bookkeeper should be the one helping you keep all the records and pay your taxes on time.

3. *Use a payroll-service company.* There are some pretty complex rules when it comes to paying the taxes associated with hiring employees. You don't want to waste your time figuring out all the rules. If you miss paying something, you will end up paying a lot of interest plus penalties. The

best option is to hire a payroll-service company and let them take care of everything for you.

Just as it pays for you to be organized, you should make sure that your employees are organized as well. If you hire your bookkeeper to design a good filing system for your business, make sure every employee is using it and following the filing procedures. As you might have noticed already, it is extremely important to have systems and procedures. You should have some kind of filing procedure and put it into the employee-training manual.

Component 6: Infrastructure

Having a good infrastructure means you have the necessary equipment for your business to function at its best. As we talk about infrastructure, ask yourself this question: "What is the current capacity of my business?" In other words, how many customers can your business handle? Given the current tools, equipment, and computers, is there a cap to how much revenue you can bring in?

Every business has a maximum capacity. Think about the number of employees you have. Think about the tools, equipment, and computers you have. If your company is busy all the time, what is the maximum amount of business you can handle right now?

The maximum amount of business you can handle is called your capacity. Now let's compare your capacity to your current revenues. Suppose your capacity is $1 million, and your revenues are currently at $1 million. What does this mean? It means that you can't grow your revenues any higher than $1 million unless you do something to increase your capacity. This could be hiring more people, buying more tools and equipment, or upgrading your computer system to make things more efficient.

Remember, your capacity is tied to your efficiency. The more efficient your work flow is, the bigger your capacity will be. That is to say, the more efficient you are, the more customers you can handle. If you want to increase your efficiency, you may or may not need to hire more people. For instance, perhaps you examine your work flow and find that there is too much verbal communication among your employees, which slows things down. To increase the amount of business you can handle, you don't necessarily need to hire more employees or buy more equipment. You might just need to redesign your work flow a bit in order to make the process more efficient.

In other words, if you want to increase your capacity, you need to somehow increase efficiency. Increasing the efficiency might involve getting a faster printer. It might involve computerizing your business. It might involve getting more or better tools and equipment. It might involve hiring more people. Or it might involve modifying your work flow to make things more efficient.

Here's another scenario. Let's say you own a trucking company that did $4 million in business last year, so you know you have the trucks and manpower to handle $4 million a year in business. What if the economy is down, and you have only $2 million in business this year? Do you fire some truck drivers? Do you sell the extra trucks you don't use? What do you do with your excess capacity? If you find yourself in a situation in which you have a lot more capacity than you have business, I believe you should focus on building your business to meet the capacity. There is always business out there. In my opinion, it comes down to laziness. You may have to stop the insurance on some trucks and set them aside for a little while, but don't sell the extra trucks. Work harder than ever to build your business back up to the $4 million mark. I've met trucking-company owners who got rid of their excess trucks when the economy was down, thinking they would contract and save money during a down economy. When the economy boomed again, they ended up scrambling because they couldn't handle the business their customers were giving them.

You want your capacity to be slightly greater than your current revenues. If your capacity is much greater than your revenues, work hard to build your revenues up. If your capacity and revenues are exactly equal, consider expanding your capacity so you can handle more business. How much greater should your capacity be in comparison with your revenues? A safe estimate is 20 percent. That means if your annual revenues are currently at $1 million, you want your capacity to be somewhere around $1.2 million a year.

As we talk about having the proper tools for your business to function at its best, remember that tools can refer to physical tools such as computers and phone lines, but it can also refer to legal tools. Having the proper legal infrastructure is just as important as having the proper physical infrastructure. The reality is that we live in a litigious society, and people sue other people all the time. If you don't have the proper legal infrastructure, you could potentially lose everything you have as the result of a lawsuit.

Earlier in the book, I recommended having an attorney as one of your essential advisors when you buy a business. Hopefully, your attorney was able to work with your CPA to give you good advice on the proper legal entities to set up. If you skipped this somehow, now is the time to put the proper legal protection in place. If you do not use an entity to run your business, you will essentially be running the business in your personal name. The problem with that is that you will be exposing yourself personally to all the potential liabilities of the business. If you have a business partner and do not set up an entity, you will be forming a general partnership by default, which means you could be personally liable for your partner's faults even if you didn't do anything wrong.

Remember that attorneys have different specialties; I recommend hiring an asset protection attorney to protect your assets. The exact entities you set up (whether it's an S-Corp, C-Corp, LLC, or something else) will depend on your particular tax situation, so have your asset protection attorney work with your CPA to put in place the proper legal protections for you.

In summary, there are six components to making your operations run smoothly: customer service, sales, collections, work-flow management, organization, and infrastructure. Focus on optimizing each of these components, and you will find your business running more efficiently and profitably.

~ INVITATION TO ACT ~

What is your biggest takeaway from this chapter?

_____

_____

_____

_____

_____

_____

~ Free Training Videos ~

Visit www.LifestyleBusinessOwner.com
to download
your free training videos on
becoming a lifestyle business owner!

CHAPTER 11

Improving the Bottom Line with Sound Financial Management

I f you are successful with your marketing efforts, you will bring in revenues. Generating revenues is only half the battle, however. There are many business owners who wonder why they don't take home much money despite the fact that their companies have high revenues.

Sound financial management allows you to translate your revenues into cash you can take home. Just having a large amount of sales is not enough. If you do not manage your cost of goods sold and operating expenses carefully, they will consume most of your revenues, leaving little net profit. And it's great if you manage to create a nice net profit, but it's still not enough. If you do not do a good job of collecting what's due to you from your customers, you may have a nice net profit on paper but little cash in your business bank account (since your customers haven't paid). And it's great if you manage to build up a nice amount of cash in your business bank account, but it's still not enough. If you spend the money impulsively (such as buying too many pieces of equipment or more inventory than you need), you could drain the bank account quickly and not have enough cash to meet the daily operational needs of the business or make a cash distribution to the owners.

Let me introduce you to the Sound Financial Management Framework:

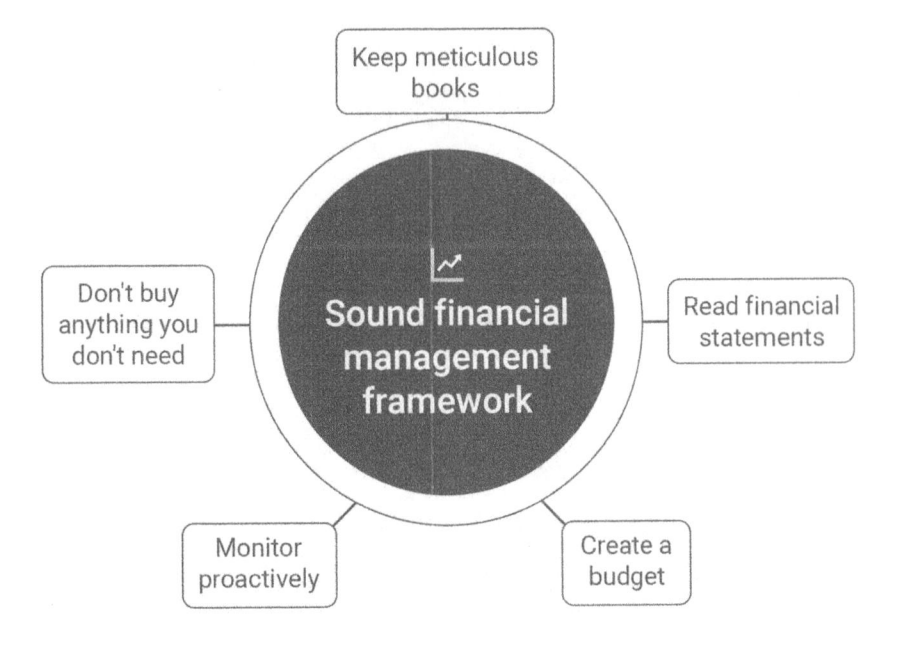

Lifestyle business owners employ these five best practices when it comes to financial management. They keep meticulous books so they know exactly how their business is doing. They read and analyze financial statements so they can catch threats as well as opportunities early. They create a budget and measure the financial performance of their company against their budget. They get into a habit of monitoring their financials proactively. Finally, they have a clear set of criteria in determining whether a purchase is worthwhile or not. Let's dive into each of these five best practices now.

Best Practice #1: Keep meticulous books. It's hard to figure out where the money goes if you do not maintain meticulous records. Some business owners prefer to do a lot of cash business (such as not reporting all of the cash income to the government or paying employees under the table using cash). Although they may seem to get ahead in the short-term by evading taxes, they will always live in fear of an audit and the inevitable day of heavy penalties will come. There are so many ways to minimize your tax obligations legally that there is really no reason to do so illegally. Incidentally, all the legal methods to minimize your tax obligations require meticulous bookkeeping and documentation. In other words, keeping good records will help you not only maximize your profits but also minimize your tax obligations. Lifestyle business owners make it a priority to keep meticulous books. If you would rather not spend your time doing bookkeeping, your money would be well spent on hiring a bookkeeping service.

Best Practice #2: Learn to read financial statements. Many business owners spend so much time operating the business that they do not take any time to evaluate how they can improve the way the business is run. Reading financial statements is a way to evaluate how your business is doing, spot dangers early, and identify opportunities to improve. Your bookkeeper can produce the financial statements for you, but it is up to you to analyze those statements and understand what they mean. If all you do is put the financial statements in a stack and never take the time to extract the message your financial statements have for you, you will miss out on many excellent opportunities to make your business more profitable.

You do not have to get a degree in accounting to understand what your financial statements are telling you. There are only three financial statements you need to learn to read, and I will give you a brief overview of what to look for in each one. The first financial statement you want to look at is the profit-and-loss statement, also called the P&L or Income Statement. The profit-and-loss statement lists your revenues followed by your expenses. If you subtract your total expenses from your total revenues, you end up with the net income (or net loss). At an intuitive level, you want your revenues to be as high as possible and expenses to be as low as possible (within reason, of course). There are some expenses you may not want to cut too much. If you reduce your marketing and advertising expenses to nothing, it could end up hurting your revenues. If you minimize your payroll expenses to the extreme by hiring the cheapest labor you can find, your business may end up producing shoddy work, upsetting customers, and hurting your revenues. Therefore, it is important to recognize where you are overspending and where you are underspending.

One of the best ways to analyze the profit-and-loss statement is by dividing every line item by your total revenues to get a percentage. For instance, if you spent $2,000 on insurance expenses and your total revenues were $100,000, then you know that 2 percent of your total revenues went to insurance. Similarly, maybe 5 percent of your total revenues went into office supplies, 20 percent of your total revenues went into paying employees, and so on and so forth. Now that you have the percentages, the key is to monitor them over time. For instance, if 2 percent of your total revenues went to paying for insurance last year and 8 percent of your total revenues went to paying for insurance this year, you might want to look closer at your insurance rates and figure out what caused the dramatic jump.

The second financial statement you want to learn to read is the balance sheet. The balance sheet lists your assets and liabilities. On an intuitive level, you know that if you take on more debt, your liabilities will increase. If you get more cash in the bank account, your assets will increase. So if you decide to borrow $20,000 from the bank, your liabilities will increase by $20,000. When you deposit the $20,000 you just borrowed into the business bank account, your cash increases by $20,000, which makes your total assets go up. In other words, your total liabilities went up by $20,000, but your total assets also went up by $20,000.

The point here is for you to get an intuitive feel of what the balance sheet is telling you. Your balance sheet tracks the amount of assets you have and the amount of debt or liabilities you have. If your cash balance is too low, your company will have trouble paying all the bills when they come due. If you have excess cash that is not needed for the daily operations of the business, you could start building up a reserve account in case an emergency happens and you need a large sum of cash, or you could save up to replace a major piece of equipment that you know will only last another three years. If you have excess cash after that, you could make an owner distribution and put money in your pocket. The cash account is a really important one to watch because the amount of cash your business has in the bank account will determine how much you can distribute to yourself, how much you can spend taking on a new initiative, and whether the company can pay its bills.

Another important account to watch on the balance sheet is your accounts receivable. If you send your customers an invoice and give them, say, thirty days or forty-five days to pay you, you will have accounts receivable. Accounts receivable is basically money that is due to your business that has not yet been collected. If your accounts receivable shows $100,000, that's $100,000 of uncollected funds. If you collected from all your customers who still haven't paid their invoices, you could have an additional $100,000 cash in the bank account. Be sure not to let your accounts receivable get too high, because it's cash you can use in your business if you get your customers to pay up.

If your business carries inventory, you will also find your inventory balance listed on the balance sheet. Having the proper amount of inventory on hand is important. If you don't have enough, you may miss out on potential sales. If you have too much inventory, however, you may find yourself low on cash because you've spent your cash buying the excess inventory, which means the cash won't be available for other purposes.

You will also find your other current assets and long-term assets listed on the balance sheet. Current assets are assets that are expected to be converted into cash within one year or less. Long-term assets are things such as business equipment, company vehicles, and property that are expected to be used for more than one year. You may also find intangible assets such as goodwill, copyrights, and patents listed on your balance sheet.

On the liabilities side of the balance sheet, you will find your current liabilities and long-term liabilities. Similar to the way assets are categorized, your current liabilities are debts and obligations due within one year, and long-term liabilities are debts and obligations due more than one year in the future. When you total up all of your assets and subtract from that figure all of your liabilities, the difference is your equity.

The third financial statement to be familiar with is the statement of cash flows. Since cash is the lifeblood of your business (and not having enough cash in the bank account will put you out of business), the statement of cash flows basically tells you whether your cash increased or decreased and how exactly it happened. The first thing you should do when you look at the statement of cash flows is to look at the very bottom. It should tell you how much cash you started with and how much cash you ended with. For instance, it could say you had $40,000 in cash at the beginning of the year and you ended up with $70,000 in cash at the end of the year. In other words, your company experienced an increase of $30,000 in cash.

The rest of the statement of cash flows explains how you got the $30,000 increase in cash. There are three sections: operating activities, investing activities, and financing activities. Operating activity refers to the cash inflows or outflows as a result of your business operations. If the $30,000 increase in cash came from operating activities, that's great news because it means you made a profit and your customers paid you, leading to an increase in cash. Investing activity refers to the cash inflow or outflow as a result of buying or selling company assets. If the $30,000 increase in cash came from investing activities, it means you sold off some equipment or company asset and got $30,000 cash in exchange. Be careful if the increase in cash is mostly explained by investing activities, because that could mean the company is going out of business and selling off all of its assets. Finally, financing activity refers to the cash inflows or outflows as a result of borrowing money or paying the owner through distributions. As you may imagine, making a distribution to the owner would decrease the company cash, and borrowing money would put cash in the company's bank account. If the increase in cash is primarily explained by financing activities, it means the company borrowed money. Is that good or bad? Well, it depends on how the money is used. If the company is borrowing money to expand operations, that could be a sign of positive things to come. If the company is struggling and borrowing money just to stay in business, it could be a danger sign.

The statement of cash flows is very telling of the health of the business. Suppose the net cash from operations is negative, the net cash from investing activities is positive, and the net cash from financing activities is positive. What does this tell you? Well, the negative net cash from operations tells you that the business is losing money (which is bad). The positive net cash from investing activities tells you that the business is selling its assets to get some short-term cash. It's like selling your TV, your bed, and your jewelry just to put food on the table. Pretty soon, you won't have anything left to sell. The positive net cash from financing activities means that the business owner is scrambling to borrow money just to cover the operations. It's like borrowing money from your relatives or anyone else who is willing to lend you money before no one is willing to lend you money anymore. Yikes! In this scenario, it doesn't matter that the overall cash balance of the company increased. The increase was a result of the wrong things, and the company is in trouble.

When you learn to read financial statements, the numbers tell a story. At our lifestyle business owner seminars, we train people on how to become extremely proficient at extracting the story out of the numbers. We hand out financial statements from real-life companies (with the company names taken out) and ask participants to tell us what the numbers are saying. Is the company doing well or is it in trouble? Where is the company doing well? What are the danger signs? Participants work in groups to figure out the message the financial statements are sending, and people are often amazed by how much they can tell about a company just by looking at a few financial statements. If you don't feel totally confident in your ability to understand financial statements, I invite you to join us at one of our training events. You will gain advanced knowledge on how to become a lifestyle business owner, meet like-minded people and make important connections, and gain clarity on what you need to do to move forward.

Best Practice #3: Create a budget every year. Several months before the start of the year, you should create a budget for the coming year. Take your profit-and-loss statement and set a goal for each line item. Let's say it is October, and you are preparing the budget for the next year. You start setting goals. In January, you plan to get $200,000 in revenues, spend $4,000 in advertising, spend $150 on insurance, spend $40,000 in payroll expenses, and so on. You go down every line item on the profit-and-loss statement until you have a target number for every line item in January. Once you are done with January, then you move on to set targets for every line item in February. Then March, April, and so on until you have a target number for every line item in every month of the coming year. That is your budget, and it is what you will measure your financial performance against.

Let's say January has come and gone, and you are comparing your January actuals with your January budget. Maybe you budgeted $200,000 in revenues, and you actually brought in $210,000. Maybe you budgeted $4,000 for advertising, but you actually spent $4,300. Maybe you budgeted $2,000 for utilities, but you actually spent $5,000. When the variance is small, you can overlook it because no one can predict the future with perfect accuracy. When the variance is large, however, you should dig deeper to find out what caused the variance. In the example above, why were your utility expenses $3,000 more than budgeted? Was there a water leak? Was the utility meter broken and you got overcharged? Having a budget in advance and comparing your actuals to the budget will allow you to catch things early. Having a budget also gives you the confidence in knowing how much you should spend on various items. If you budgeted $4,000 for advertising and then you learned that putting an ad on a bus would cost $10,000, you can pass on the opportunity. Conversely, if you budgeted $4,000 and you've only spent $200, you know you should increase your advertising spending.

Best Practice #4: Proactively monitor the financials. Many business owners ask how they can tell whether a number on their financial statement is good or bad. If they spent $5,000 on marketing, is that good or bad? Lifestyle business owners know that there are three ways to tell whether a number is good or bad. First, you compare it to the budget. If only $3,000 is budgeted for marketing, then you know the actual spending of $5,000 is high. Second, you compare the number to your company's historical performance. If you spent $5,000 in January 2017, how much did you spend on marketing in January 2016 and January 2015? You can also look at percentages. If 5 percent of your total income was spent on marketing in January 2017, what percentage of your income was spent on marketing in January 2016 and January 2015? Finally, you can compare your financials to the industry averages. Every industry is different, and there are industry-specific reports and consultants who can tell you what the industry averages are.

Lifestyle business owners monitor their company's performance daily, weekly, monthly, quarterly, and yearly. Are revenues trending up or trending down? Are expenses trending up or trending down? How do the actual revenues and expenses compare to the budgeted revenues and expenses? Are there large variances that require further research and corrective action? How do the company's financial ratios compare with those of the industry? For your industry, do you know what percentage of your revenues should go to the cost of labor? What percentage of your revenues should go to the cost of parts? What percentage of your revenues should end up in the owner's pocket? The sooner you catch a negative trend, the sooner you can adjust. By understanding their industry and monitoring their financials carefully, lifestyle business owners can fine-tune their business to maximize profitability.

Now I will share with you six important ratios you can use to measure the performance of your company.

Return on Assets (ROA)

The first efficiency measure I will introduce to you is the most important one. It's called Return on Assets, or ROA for short. It is calculated as follows:

$$\text{Return on Assets} = \frac{\text{Owner's Discretionary Income}}{\text{Total Assets}}$$

Let's use an example to demonstrate how the return on assets is used. Suppose my business makes $200,000 a year (meaning my ODI is $200,000 a year), and my business requires $1,600,000 of assets to generate this much profit. My ROA would be $200,000/$1,600,000 = 12.5%. Let's say your business also makes $200,000 in ODI, but your business requires only $300,000 in assets. Your ROA would be $200,000/$300,000 = 66.7%. This means your business is a lot more efficient than mine is.

The ROA measures the overall efficiency of your company. The higher it is, the more efficient your company is. A high number is good, and a low number is bad. You want your ROA to be increasing over time.

So how do you increase your ROA over time? You have to understand what it is made of. The ROA is made up of two components: profit margin and asset turnover. I will explain these two components next.

Profit Margin

Profit margin is the first component of ROA. It is calculated as follows:

$$Profit\ Margin = \frac{Owner's\ Discretionary\ Income}{Total\ Revenues}$$

If your ODI is $200,000 and your total revenues are $1,000,000, your profit margin would be $\$200,000/\$1,000,000 = 20\%$.

The profit margin tells you how much of the total revenues you bring in ends up in the owner's pocket. A high number is good; a low number is bad. As a lifestyle business owner, I like to see the profit margin at 15% or higher.

Asset Turnover

Asset turnover is the second component of ROA. It is calculated as follows:

$$Asset\ Turnover = \frac{Total\ Revenues}{Total\ Assets}$$

If your total revenues are $1,000,000 and your total assets are $1,600,000, your asset turnover would be $\$1,000,000/\$1,600,000 = 62.5\%$.

The asset turnover measures how intensely you are employing your assets to generate revenues. A high number is good, and a low number is bad. If your asset turnover is high, people call it "quick asset turnover." If your asset turnover is low, people call it "slow asset turnover."

Let me now explain how the profit margin and asset turnover are put together to give you your ROA.

$$Profit\ Margin = \frac{ODI}{Total\ Revenues}$$

$$Asset\ Turnover = \frac{Total\ Revenues}{Total\ Assets}$$

When you multiply these two ratios together, you get:

$$Profit\ Margin \times Asset\ Turnover = \frac{ODI}{Total\ Revenues} \times \frac{Total\ Revenues}{Total\ Assets} = \frac{ODI}{Total\ Assets} = ROA$$

As you can see, the total revenues cancel out, and you get ROA as a result. In other words, the ROA is simply the profit margin and asset turnover multiplied together. The higher your profit margin is, the higher your ROA is. The higher your asset turnover is, the higher your ROA is. If you want to increase your ROA, which is the overall efficiency of your company, you have to either increase your profit margin or increase your asset turnover.

Usually, your profit margin and asset turnover are negatively correlated. What this means is that if you want to pursue a high profit margin, you generally have to sacrifice a little on asset turnover. If you want a high asset turnover, you generally have to sacrifice on your profit margin. Let me show you what I mean.

A doctor's office makes good profit margins, because the doctor gets paid well to see each patient. But a doctor's office tends to have low asset turnover, because there is a limit to how many patients the doctor can see. Walmart, though, has really thin margins on its products. It makes only a few dollars here and there from the products it sells. But it has a really high asset turnover. Imagine the volume of products it sells. The few dollars here and there start to accumulate, which makes Walmart extremely profitable. Both the doctor's office and Walmart are really efficient companies (meaning they both have a high ROA), but they are efficient in different ways. The doctor's office achieves its high ROA through pursuing a high profit margin, while Walmart achieves its high ROA through a high asset turnover.

Which strategy should you pursue? Should you aim for a high profit margin or a high asset turnover? It depends on the type of business you own. Personally, I prefer to focus on the high profit margin. As you know, I like to buy businesses in the service industry. In my experience, it is much easier to get a high profit margin than it is to get a high asset turnover. Most owners of small service businesses don't charge their customers enough. They think that if they charge more, they will lose customers. The truth is that customers are willing to pay more if your customer service is good enough. By providing excellent customer service and quality work, you will be able to charge more, which will increase your profit margin. Once you achieve a great profit margin, then work on increasing revenues.

Collections Period

Your collections period measures the number of days it takes for your customers to pay you. It tells you how good you are at collecting money from people. Let's say your accounts receivable policy gives customers 10 days to pay. Suppose we calculate your collections period, and it turns out to be 22. That means, on average, your customers take 22 days to pay you. That's not good. Your collections period should be 10 or close to 10, if your policy states that you give people 10 days to pay.

Here's how to calculate your collections period:

$$\text{Collections Period} = \frac{\text{Accounts Receivable}}{(\text{Total Revenues}/365)}$$

Having the parentheses at the bottom means you calculate that part first. You would divide your total revenues by 365 first, and then divide the result into accounts receivable. Let's say your accounts receivable is $80,000, and your total revenues are $1,000,000. Here's how the collections period would be calculated:

$$\text{Collections Period} = \frac{\text{Accounts Receivable}}{(\text{Total Revenues}/365)} = \frac{\$80,000}{\$1,000,000/365} = \frac{\$80,000}{\$2,739.73} = 29.2 \text{ days}$$

In this example, the business takes on average 29.2 days to collect money from its customers.

The collections period is sometimes called "Days Sales Outstanding." Your collections period should be close to or less than your accounts receivable policy. If you give people 10 days to pay you, your collections period should come close to 10 or be less than 10.

Days Sales in Cash

Days sales in cash is a measure of how much cash you keep in the bank account compared to how much sales you do. It is calculated as follows:

$$\text{Days Sales in Cash} = \frac{\text{Cash}}{(\text{Total Revenues}/365)}$$

If this number is high, it means you have too much cash in your bank account, and the cash is not being put to efficient use. Therefore, you want this ratio to be low, but not too low. If this number gets too low, it means you don't have enough cash to cover your operations, and your business might be in trouble.

What is considered high, what is considered low, and what is considered too low? Well, that is going to vary with each business. Your business mentor can help you determine the ideal amount of cash to keep in your business bank account. Suppose you are currently making $1,000,000 a year in total revenues, and the ideal amount of cash to have in your bank account is $50,000. Your ideal days sales in cash would be calculated as follows:

$$\text{Days Sales in Cash} = \frac{Cash}{(Total\ Revenues/365)} = \frac{\$50,000}{\$1,000,000/365} = \frac{\$50,000}{\$2,739.73} = 18.25\ days$$

That means your target is to keep your days sales in cash around 18.25. As your business grows, you will need to keep more cash in the business bank account to ensure smooth operations. In the example above, if your business were to double and your total revenues became $2,000,000 per year, you would need to keep $100,000 cash in the bank in order to maintain your days sales in cash at 18.25.

Quick Ratio

The quick ratio measures your company's ability to meet its short-term obligations. You basically compare your short-term assets with your short-term liabilities to see which one is greater. If your short-term assets are greater, that means your company is in good shape. If your short-term assets are less than your short-term liabilities, you might be in trouble. Here's how the quick ratio is calculated:

$$\text{Quick Ratio} = \frac{Cash + Accounts\ Receivable}{Total\ Current\ Liabilities}$$

If your cash account has $60,000, your accounts receivable has $70,000, and your total current liabilities are $100,000, your quick ratio would be:

$$Quick\ Ratio = \frac{Cash + Accounts\ Receivable}{Total\ Current\ Liabilities} = \frac{\$60,000 + \$70,000}{\$100,000} = \frac{\$130,000}{\$100,000} = 1.3$$

A quick ratio of 1.5 is excellent. A quick ratio of 1 means you are doing okay. A quick ratio of less than 1 means you might be in trouble. The quick ratio tells you whether you have enough cash and accounts receivable (which can be converted into cash fairly quickly) to pay the people that need to be paid.

What we are measuring is your company's solvency, which is your company's ability to pay the people that need to be paid (including banks, creditors, government, employees, vendors, and so on). If your quick ratio is above 1, it means your company is healthy. It means you have enough short-term assets to meet your obligations as they come due.

Best Practice #5: Don't buy anything you don't need. As you know, controlling your expenses is extremely important if you want to keep your company profitable. Are you spending your money in the right places? How can you tell if you are wasting money or making a good purchase decision?

Here's the principle: every purchase decision has to make your business more profitable. A very common mistake business owners make is buying too many pieces of equipment. Every time you are faced with a decision to buy or not buy something, you have to ask yourself, "Do I absolutely need this right now? Can my business do without it? Is this going to help me increase revenues? Why?"

Let's go through a few examples to show you how a purchase decision should be made. Suppose you are considering the purchase of a piece of equipment that costs $10,000. If you buy this, you estimate that your revenues will increase by $600 a month. Should you buy this piece of equipment or not?

The first thing you should do is to figure out how long it will take you to recoup the cost of the equipment. If your revenues increase by $600 a month, how much of it is contributing to profits? This is where you look at your gross margin. If you look at your profit-and-loss statement, your gross margin is calculated as follows:

$$Gross\ Margin = \frac{Gross\ Profit}{Total\ Revenues}$$

If your revenues are $500,000 and your gross profit is $300,000, your gross margin would be $300,000 / $500,000, or 60%. If your gross margin is 60%, it means that when you make $600 in revenues, 60% of that is contributing to your profits. In our example, the $10,000 piece of equipment would increase your revenues by $600 a month, which means that it would increase your profits by $360 a month. The $360 is calculated by $600 60%.

Let's now calculate how long it would take to recoup the cost of your equipment investment. In other words, if you make an additional $360 a month, how long would it take for you just to pay for the initial cost of your investment? You take $10,000 / $360, which gives you 27.78 months. That's about 28 months, which is 2 years and 4 months. If you spend $10,000 to make an additional $360 a month, it would take you 2 years and 4 months just to recoup the cost of your initial $10,000. After 2 years and 4 months, you will start to put an additional $360 a month into your pocket.

Here's the question: if it takes you 2 years and 4 months to recoup the cost of your investment, is that good or bad? In my opinion, it is very bad.

If an investment takes you 2 to 5 years just to recoup the cost, it is a terrible investment. A good investment should take you 1 to 2 months to recoup the cost. If an investment takes you 6 to 12 months to recoup the cost, you should start to question whether it is really worth it.

Let's do another example. Let's say you are considering buying something that costs you $10,000. If you buy it, you estimate that it will increase your revenues by $9,000 a month. You look at your profit-and-loss statement and see that your revenues are $600,000 and your gross profit is $400,000. Should you buy it or not?

Well, let's calculate your gross margin. Your gross margin would be $400,000 / $600,000, or 66.7%. That means if your revenues increase by $9,000 a month, 66.7% of that, or $6,000, would become profits. Now the question becomes should you spend $10,000 to make an additional $6,000 a month? Well, let's see how long it would take you to recoup the cost of your investment. Take $10,000

/ $6,000, which gives you 1.67 months, which is a little bit more than a month and a half. Is this a good investment? Absolutely! Any investment that takes 1-2 months to recoup the cost is a great investment. You should definitely buy this.

Do you see the logic we are using? Every time you consider buying something, you have to see whether the purchase gives you an adequate return. Just because buying something would make your business more profitable doesn't mean you should buy it. You have to be able to recoup your cost within a few months.

At this point, you may be asking: how do you estimate how much more business you will get as a result of buying something? For instance, how do you estimate that if you buy a new tool, your revenues will increase by $9,000 a month? Well, some things are easier to estimate than others. Let's say you currently have to turn away 20 customers a month because you lack this tool. You look at how much each customer spends on average at your business. Let's say that, on average, your customer spends $450 during each visit. This means if you turn away 20 customers a month because you lack this tool, you are turning away $9,000 of business a month, since 20 $450 = $9,000. If you had this tool, you would make an additional $9,000 in revenues, which would translate into $6,000 in gross profit (assuming that your gross margin was 66.7%). If this tool costs $10,000, it would be a very good investment.

Let's say a salesperson comes in the door and shows you how to put your company logo on pens and key tags. The first questions you should ask yourself are: "Is having my company logo on pens and key tags really going to increase revenues? Will this bring in more business for me? How many more customers will do business with me because I now have my company logo on pens and key tags?" Well, if you really think about it, pens and key tags probably won't bring in many more sales for you, if any at all. Therefore, buying pens and key tags is probably a waste of money.

Now that you understand that your purchases have to make your business more profitable within a reasonable period of time, let me add another layer to this discussion. It is important to pay attention to the image of your business. Remember that marketing is how your customers perceive you. In other words, you want to give your customers a pleasant experience from start to finish. If the customer bathroom in your lobby is dirty and old, remodeling the bathroom alone probably won't increase revenues, but remodeling the bathroom along with improving the image of your business in many other ways will lead to more revenues. Let's say your company has a few vehicles that are used to deliver products to your customers. Keeping these vehicles washed on a regular basis may not increase revenues, but it will improve the image of your business. The point I am making here is that one single action to improve your image probably won't increase revenues, but many actions taken together to improve your image will increase revenues. Therefore, spending money to create a good image is still a good idea.

When you buy something, make sure you are not stretching your limits just to buy it. In other words, if you don't have $10,000, don't stretch yourself just to buy a $10,000 piece of equipment. You can always buy it later when you have more cash available. When it comes to making purchase decisions, be frugal and weigh your returns. Figure out the pros and cons, and don't waste your money. Remember, the most common mistake business owners make is buying too much, not buying too little.

We are now reaching the end of this chapter, so let's recap. There are five best practices lifestyle business owners employ in sound financial management: they keep meticulous books, they read financial statements, they use a budget to manage their income and expenses, they proactively monitor their financials, and they don't buy anything they don't need. If you employ these best practices, you will see your bottom line increase over time, which will set you up to work fewer hours and become a lifestyle business owner.

As you know, there are three steps in the Lifestyle Business Owner Formula. Step one is to buy a good business. Step two is to increase its profits. We have now covered the four ways to increase your profits: smart marketing, effective employee management, smooth operations, and sound financial management. In the next section, I will guide you through step three in the Lifestyle Business Owner Formula, which is to empower your people. You see, everything we've done so far is to set you up to become a lifestyle business owner. Without buying a good business, you could spend years just trying to get your business off the ground. Without enough profits, you won't be able to afford hiring a manager so you can work fewer hours. Now that you have purchased a solid business as a foundation and increased its profits, it's time to show you how to actually step back and become a lifestyle business owner. Congratulate yourself for getting this far, and I will see you in the next chapter!

~ INVITATION TO ACT ~
What is your biggest takeaway from this chapter?

_____

_____

_____

_____

_____

~ Free Training Videos ~
Visit www.LifestyleBusinessOwner.com
to download
your free training videos on
becoming a lifestyle business owner!

PART IV

How to Become a Lifestyle Business Owner

Lifestyle Business Owner Formula		3 Empower your people
	2 Increase profits	
	1 Buy a good business	

CHAPTER 12

What Does Becoming a Lifestyle Business Owner Mean?

Every time I talk with business owners, they are fascinated by the concept of owning a lifestyle business. How do you set up a business to run by itself without you having to be there? How can you trust that your employees will do a good job when you are not there? What if your business doesn't run right when you leave? In this chapter, I want to share with you what it means to be a lifestyle business owner and what you must do if you want to own a business that can run without your daily presence.

Life as a Lifestyle Business Owner

What is it like to be a lifestyle business owner? There are four traits that lifestyle business owners share. First, the business is designed around their values and priorities. They run the business instead of the business running them. They decide what's important to them and make sure the business fits into the lifestyle they want to live.

Second, lifestyle business owners have freedom with their time. Just about all the lifestyle business owners I meet value work-life balance and choose to work less than a full-time schedule. I've met lifestyle business owners who work ten hours a week, fifteen hours a week, or twenty hours a week. At a minimum, they spend five hours a week monitoring their business, but this could be done on-site or off-site. The business runs by itself for the most part, so the owners are free to do whatever they want with their time. If done right, being a lifestyle business owner means more freedom and less stress.

Third, lifestyle business owners run their businesses with a different set of standards than most other business owners. As a lifestyle business owner, you have to accept what is less than perfection in your eyes. No one cares about your business as much as you do, and that's okay. You can still run a profitable business even if your employees don't run everything to the level of perfection you demand. If you want everything to be run perfectly, chances are you will end up being at your business every day looking over everything. You can set up systems so that things will be done mostly right without you being there. But once you take off, things will probably never be done to the level of perfection you demand. Having to accept what is less than perfection in your eyes is the price you pay to become a lifestyle business owner. I learned this lesson the hard way myself. When I became the co-owner of the truck-washing business at the age of eighteen, I wanted perfection. I had such high standards for how clean the trucks needed to be that I would end up overseeing the crew myself. A fleet of trucks that should've taken two hours to wash ended up taking four hours to wash. I was stressed out, my truck washers were stressed out, and the company couldn't take on more business because every job took twice as long as it should to get done. Finally, after getting pressure from my business partner, I backed off. I realized that what was "midlevel service" in my mind was still way better than the service offered by my competitors. What was even more surprising to me was that the customers were happy with what I considered "midlevel service." I tried to demand perfection but ended up creating a negative situation. When I let go, my employees were happier, I ended up with more free time, the customers were still happy, and the company was able to get more accounts.

The fourth and final trait that lifestyle business owners have in common is that they have to accept making less money for a while in most cases. Let's say you currently make $150,000 a year as an owner-operator. To become a lifestyle business owner, you'll need to hire a manager to run the daily operations. Suppose the going rate for a manager in your industry is $45,000 a year, and you decide to pay $50,000 a year for a top-notch manager. That leaves you with $100,000 a year. Would you be happy making $100,000 a year? If the answer is yes, congratulations! You can hire a manager, step away, and make the income you need. What if you need to make more than $100,000 a year? Sometimes it's a good idea to take one step back so you can take ten steps forward. Maybe you sacrifice a little bit and live on only $100,000 a year for a while. What you have gained in return is free time. You can use this time to build your business. As Michael Gerber says in *The E-Myth Revisited,* there is a big difference between working in your business and working on your business. You may be working in your business every day, but you are not necessarily making your business better. When you have the free time to work on your business, you can take your business to the next level. Sooner or later, you may be making $150,000 a year or more as a lifestyle business owner. You can even use your free time to buy a second business and become a lifestyle business owner in the second business. The possibilities are endless when you have the free time to be creative.

Five Ways to Become a Lifestyle Business Owner

As you contemplate the idea of lifestyle business ownership, you need to consider two things: what do you want to do with your time and how much money do you really need to live? The answers to these two questions will determine how you will become a lifestyle business owner.

As it turns out, there are five ways you can become a lifestyle business owner. Take a look and see which one is right for you.

1. *Step away completely and accept a lower income.* People who choose this option generally have this in common: they don't like working in their business. They are okay with accepting a lower income, and they have so many more things they would rather do with their time. If this sounds like you, turn your business into a lifestyle business owner operation, and take off!

2. *Step away completely and spend your time acquiring more businesses and investments.* People who choose this option generally want complete freedom with their time but don't want to compromise on their income. They are ambitious at heart. They want to be wealthy, and they are interested in owning multiple sources of income. They are interested in business and investing, and they want to spend their time acquiring and systemizing businesses and investments.

3. *Own several businesses of the same kind.* What I mean here is that if you own a massage therapy business, own several of them. If you own an Italian restaurant, own several of them. People who choose this option generally enjoy working in their business but want freedom. They work because they choose to, not because they have to. Suppose you enjoy being a massage therapist, but you want the ability to take off whenever you want. Well, you could own several massage therapy businesses and let them provide the income that you need. Then you would have the ability to give massages whenever you want and still make the income you need without being required to give massages on a full-time basis.

4. *Step away halfway.* You don't have to completely step away from your business. You can simply reduce your work hours by half. People who choose this option would like to have more time, but they would be bored if they suddenly had nothing to do. What's more, they enjoy doing what they do; they just want to have a little bit more time and freedom. They are willing to reduce their income a little bit by hiring a part-time manager, but they are not willing to reduce their income too much by hiring a full-time one. If this sounds like you, stepping away halfway might be the right option for you.

5. *Switching careers.* Perhaps you do not enjoy working in your business anymore, and you want to do something else. You could sell your business and do something else, or you could turn your current business into a lifestyle business owner operation and then go do something else. Which option you go with will depend on how quickly you want to get out. If you want to get out now, you might consider selling your business. In the world of small business, you make your money running

the business, not selling it. This means your business probably won't sell for as much as you would like it to, but letting it go might be the right option for your life right now. If you are willing to stick it out and spend another year systemizing your business, you could turn it into a lifestyle business owner operation, keep the income stream, and then take off to pursue a different career. Something to consider is that becoming a lifestyle business owner doesn't mean you will be worry-free. You still need to spend five hours a week maintaining your business and making sure that things are running smoothly. If this is something you don't want to do, selling the business and doing something else might be the better option for you.

Top Obstacles to Lifestyle Business Ownership

What holds most people back from becoming lifestyle business owners? The answer is very simple: fear. Most business owners are afraid that their business will not run right if they take off. Let's explore the three most common fears of lifestyle business ownership:

1. *Your employees don't care about your business as much as you do.* This fear is true. Even the employees of lifestyle business owners do not care about the business as much as the owners do. This doesn't prevent people from becoming lifestyle business owners. You can still own a profitable business as a lifestyle business owner even if your employees don't care about your business as much as you do. Your employees will make mistakes and mess up sometimes. That's why I say you have to accept what is less than perfection in your eyes.

2. *Your employees will run your business into the ground.* Your employees will only run your business into the ground if you don't set up systems and procedures and don't monitor your business on a regular basis. When you write your employee-training manuals, you are establishing step-by-step procedures for how the job duties are to be performed. If you monitor your business on a regular basis, you will know if your employees are breaking the procedures. You need to hold your employees accountable

to following the procedures. You are open to revising the procedures if there is a better way of doing something, but once the procedures are revised, you need to hold your employees accountable to the new procedures. Being a lifestyle business owner doesn't mean letting your employees have complete freedom to do whatever they want. Before you leave, you set up systems and procedures so there is a standardized method for every part of your business. After you leave, you continue to monitor your business to make sure things are running fine. If something major goes wrong, you return right away to correct it until it is right again. If something minor goes wrong, you let your manager handle it. If you empower your employees by creating a great work environment and giving them the tools and training they need to succeed, they will do a good job even when you are no longer there.

3. *Customers come because they want to see the owner.* If this is the case for your business, it means you haven't properly systemized it. Why do customers like to see you? Is it because you are friendly? What is it that you do that makes the customers want to come? Write down these behaviors and train your employees on them. Sometimes you might be surprised that customers come anyway, even when you are not there. You might lose a few customers by stepping away, but is the loss really enough to worry you? Perhaps the majority of your customers continue to come even when you are not there. You never want your customers to come just because they like your personality. You want them to come because your business consistently provides excellent customer service. If it is friendliness, you can train your employees on friendliness. If it's the fact that you are diligent on your follow-through, you can train your employees to be diligent on follow-through. Whatever it is that is causing your customers to come, you need to transfer that skill to your employees. The truth is that what customers want is pretty universal. They want friendly service, quality work, good communication, good prices, and so on. Set up your system so you can deliver these things to your customers.

The Formula for Making Your Business Run without You

Here is a very successful formula that my high-level clients have learned from me:

Address your fears + manager + systems = Business that runs without you

Let me explain the three parts of this formula. First, you must address your fears. You must learn to trust your employees, have realistic expectations, and know that your business can run well even when you are not there.

Second, you need to hire a good manager. If all you do is hire a manager, however, the manager might run the business his or her way. That's why you need the third part of the formula: implementing systems. Remember the employee-training manuals? They spell out your policies and how each job should be done step-by-step. You must write a manual not only for your current employees but also for your manager, teaching him or her how to manage your business. When you have a standardized method for every task and you hold people accountable to these procedures, your business will start to function in a consistent manner.

How to Hire a Great Manager

We have talked previously about addressing your fears and setting up systems. Now I want to talk about how you hire a great manager. All the recommendations I gave previously on attracting and keeping the best talent still apply. Here are some additional guidelines on what to look for in a manager. Ideally, you want someone who has experience as a manager, preferably in your industry. Your first choice is someone who has been a manager in your industry for many years and has a track record of bringing in great sales numbers. Sometimes you might have to hire a manager from a different industry and train him or her on the ins and outs of your industry. What you do not want is someone who has never managed people before, even if this person has been working in your industry for many years. Knowing your industry is one thing, but the ability to manage people is something else. It is often easier to teach someone about the industry than it is to teach someone how to manage people. When you look for a manager, you want someone with a lot of experience managing people and, if possible, you want that person to know about your industry as well.

Other qualities to look for in a great manager include confidence and the willingness to listen. You need a manager who is confident enough to manage your staff and make decisions yet humble enough to learn and listen so he or she follows your systems and doesn't run the business his or her own way.

So where do you find a great manager? You can find a great manager from several sources, which I discuss in the following list.

- *Referrals.* A good way to begin is to ask around. Who do you know that is looking for a job as a manager? Since referrals come from the people you trust, the quality of the people you get from them tends to be good. You never know what you'll hear when you keep your ears open. Ask around, and you might just find a great manager.
- *Craigslist.* Just as you can find good employees from Craigslist, you can also find good managers here. Post a job ad for free or for a very small fee (depending on the city you are in), and you may be surprised by the response you get.
- *Post a classified ad.* You can post a classified ad in the local metropolitan newspaper or on job-search sites such as Monster.com, Indeed.com, CareerBuilder.com, or GlassDoor.com. You can get some good responses if the ad is done right.
- *Your competitors.* Sometimes you can walk into your competitor's business and ask the manager if he or she is interested in working for you instead. It doesn't have to be your direct competitor. Today, lots of people have LinkedIn profiles. You can search and browse people's LinkedIn profiles and contact them directly to see whether they might be interested in a career change.
- *Hiring agency.* Hiring agencies are another good place to go for hiring managers. I have found that some hiring agencies are great to work with, and the money spent on them is well worth the time and effort that goes into finding a good manager.

Having a great manager will make your life a lot easier, but keep in mind that you might have to try out a few managers before you find the right one. It will take some time to find the right manager, but the effort is well worth it.

To keep a great manager, I recommend paying your manager a little above the going rate. Every business has a going rate for a manager. If you pay a little above the going rate, you will be able to attract and retain a top-notch manager. This is money well spent.

It is often a good idea to offer the manager some kind of commission if the sales exceed a certain level. Suppose your current sales are $100,000 per month. A goal of $120,000 per month in sales is a reasonable target, and a goal of $140,000 per month in sales would be a stretch. The incentive program could look something like this: in addition to the base salary, if sales for the month exceed $120,000, your manager will get 1.5 percent of sales above $100,000 as additional pay. If sales for the month exceed $140,000, the manager will get 2 percent of sales above $100,000 as additional pay. Do you think your manager will work hard to make sure he or she at least hits $120,000 a month in sales? You bet! The more money the business makes, the more money your manager makes. This is a win-win situation.

When setting up incentive programs, consider setting two targets: a realistic target and an ambitious target. If you are starting the incentive program for the first time, let the manager know that you will review how well the program is working in three months, and you reserve the right to change the numbers if necessary to make it work better. If $120,000 a month in sales turns out to be too big a stretch, you might want to lower the target. If it turns out to be too easy, you reserve the right to raise the target. After the first review, you can review it every six months. Do your homework first to make sure what you offer is what you can deliver. Don't lower your manager's guaranteed base salary when you introduce the incentive program. Finally, put the incentive program in writing. By following these guidelines, you will be on your way to attracting and retaining a great manager.

Common Mistakes When Becoming a Lifestyle Business Owner

There are many mistakes people make when they try to become lifestyle business owners, but some are more common than others. I want to highlight two of the most common mistakes so you can prevent them from happening.

Mistake 1: Not having a good manager in place. When you step away, your customers' perception of your business will largely depend on how your manager handles daily situations. In many cases, your manager will be wearing two hats: the hat of a salesperson and the hat of a manager. Your manager will be making sales and interacting with the customers as well as managing employee issues and handling the day-to-day operations of the business. You need a good manager who works hard to provide excellent customer service. You need a good manager who follows your system and listens to you.

The mistake business owners make is that they are so eager to leave that they do not select a manager that is good enough. Keep in mind that you may have to try out several managers before you step away. Even when you have found the right manager, you still have to work side by side with this new manager for a while until he or she really knows your expectations and is completely trained on how your business runs. Select your manager carefully according to the criteria I've talked about in this chapter. Not everyone can be a manager.

Mistake 2: Not giving the manager enough responsibility. Another mistake business owners often make is being too scared to delegate. Ever heard the saying that "if you want things done right, do it yourself"? Well, as a lifestyle business owner, you cannot apply this saying to your business. You need to delegate—even if your manager can't do it as well as you can. Being a lifestyle business owner means being willing to train your manager. Instead of taking charge and doing it yourself (because you are used to it and you are so good at it), you may need to let your manager do it and make a few mistakes so that he or she can learn.

Sometimes failure is the best teacher. When you train your manager, you can't try to protect him or her from making mistakes. You do your best to train, but you've got to give your manager some room to mess up and fail. When that happens, you are there to help and train some more. Don't be so scared of your manager's mistakes that you end up doing everything yourself and not giving your manager enough responsibility. Relax. Learn to trust people. You'll be surprised that your manager and your employees can do a good job even when you are not there.

How to Monitor Your Business as a Lifestyle Business Owner

By now, you've heard me say many times that even the most absentee lifestyle business owners spend a minimum of five hours a week on their businesses. So what do they do during these five hours? Here's a list of what you might do:

- Marketing—you might be reviewing the effectiveness of your advertising, designing a new marketing campaign, and making marketing decisions for the company.
- Financial review—reviewing the numbers for your business is going to take some time. Make sure that everything is in line.
- Payroll—when you first become a lifestyle business owner, I recommend that you still input the payroll yourself. Your employees will give you the hours they have worked or billed, and you will input these numbers into the system that the payroll company gives you (you either call up a representative, fax it in, e-mail it in, or enter it online). Inputting the payroll yourself ensures that no employee just gives himself or herself a raise or big bonus. You don't have to input the payroll yourself forever, but I recommend you start here.
- Purchasing decisions—there might be some major purchases that need to be made. In the preceding chapter, I went into great detail about how to determine whether or not you should make a major purchase.
- Employee management—chances are there will be some employee issues at some point. You can let your manager handle most of them, but sometimes you will need to step in and work out any major issues.

Time Frame to Become a Lifestyle Business Owner

How long does it take to become a lifestyle business owner? It largely depends on what point your business is at now and how much money you need to live on.

Does your business generate enough profits to support your personal expenses after you hire a manager? If not, you'll need to either build up your business or reduce your personal expenses.

In general, it takes about one year for most business owners to become lifestyle business owners. During this year, you will build your sales and profits up to the next level, systemize your operations, and hire a manager. If your business is already profitable enough to hire a manager or your personal expenses are low, this will speed up the process.

Note that when I say it generally takes one year, I am referring to businesses that have been established, not start-up businesses. For start-up businesses, it generally takes four years to become a lifestyle business owner, since it takes a while to establish your business to the point at which you have consistent sales and cash flow.

This is a major reason I prefer to buy existing businesses and turn them into lifestyle business owner operations rather than starting new businesses. It takes too long to turn a start-up business into a lifestyle business owner operation, and it is often a lot riskier. Given the high failure rate of start-ups, who knows if your start-up business will even last four years?

As the owner of an existing business, give yourself one year, give or take a few months, to become a lifestyle business owner. Have realistic expectations, and I am confident that you will reach your goals.

~ INVITATION TO ACT ~
What is your biggest takeaway from this chapter?

_____

_____

_____

_____

_____

_____

~ Free Training Videos ~
Visit www.LifestyleBusinessOwner.com
to download
your free training videos on
becoming a lifestyle business owner!

CHAPTER 13

How to Think Like a
Lifestyle Business Owner

In the last chapter, I gave you an overview of the process to become a lifestyle business owner. In this chapter, I want to show you how lifestyle business owners think. People often ask me, "Aaron, what exactly do lifestyle business owners do? What actions do they take?" Although understanding what lifestyle business owners do is important, understanding how they think is even more important. If you can understand their thinking process, the actions to take will follow naturally.

I've spent many years studying how lifestyle business owners think. For the first time, I am revealing what I call the Smart-Thinking Framework. I've found that there are five main differences between the way lifestyle business owners think and the way ordinary business owners think. If you can absorb these five principles, you will catapult your life and your business to the next level. Without further ado, here is the Smart-Thinking Framework:

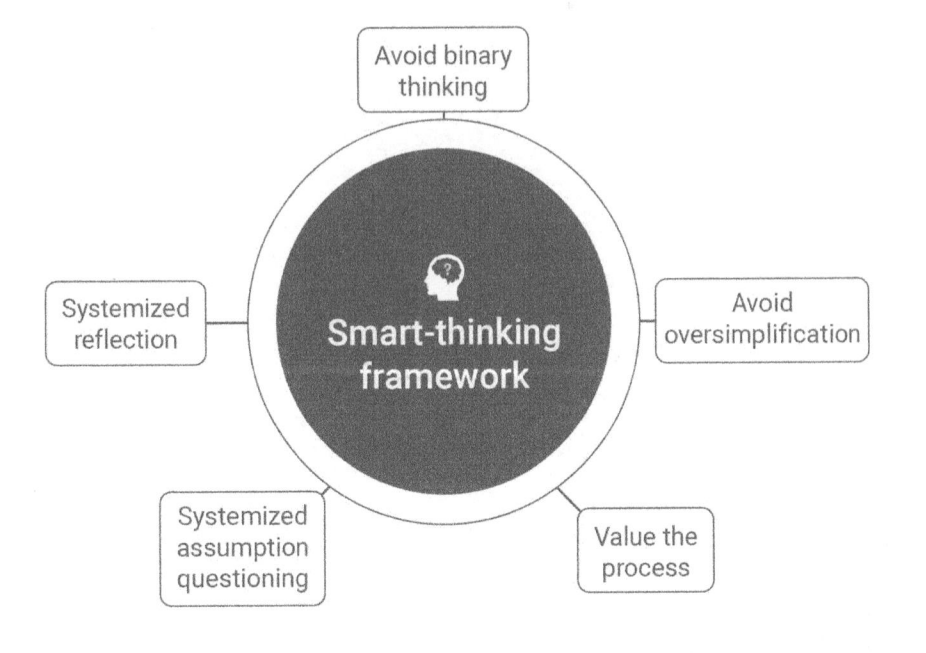

Principle 1: Avoid binary thinking. The entire Information Age is built on computers, which are binary. You get either a 1 or a 0. Living in the Information Age, it's hard not to be surrounded by binary thinking. Binary thinking is when you force yourself to choose between 1 or 0. In other words, you artificially force yourself to choose between two options, A or B. You can either have A or have B. It's a very mechanistic way of thinking.

Let me give you some examples of binary thinking:

- "I can either make my employees happy or run a profitable business."
- "I can either have a well-run business or have work-life balance."
- "I must accomplish X before I can do Y." For instance, "I must make a lot of money before I can do good in the world."

The problem with binary thinking is that it forces us to think the way machines do. Humans are holistic. We are creative. We can innovate and think outside the box. By thinking in an either/or manner, we are limiting our creativity and making a false choice.

Lifestyle business owners do their best to avoid binary thinking. Instead of feeling forced to have either A or B, they ask themselves, "How can I have both?" For instance, "How can I make my employees happy *and* run a profitable business at the same time?" or "How can I have a well-run business *and* work-life balance?" Instead of thinking they must make a lot of money before they can do good in the world, they think about how they can *do both* now.

Binary thinking tends to take the form of *either/or* statements. For instance, "*Either* I can make a lot of money, *or* I can do good in the world." Lifestyle business owners don't believe in these false choices. They think in terms of *both/and*. For instance, "How can I have *both* A *and* B? How can I *both* make a lot of money *and* do good in the world?"

When you think in terms of *both/and*, you open your mind to possibilities and innovation. This is key to building a lifestyle business, because you will need to innovate and create new solutions as you become a lifestyle business owner.

Principle 2: Avoid oversimplification. We live in a complex world, and it is often easier for our brains to put labels on things in order to better manage all the information that comes at us. These labels often come in the form of *good* or *bad*. We label something as good, or we label something as bad. Once we assign a label, we can stop thinking about the issue because we now know what it means. Let me give you some examples:

- "Government regulations are bad."
- "Government regulations are good."
- "Business is evil."
- "Business is good."
- "Capitalism is good."
- "Capitalism is bad."
- "Republicans are good."
- "Republicans are bad."
- "Military spending is good."
- "Military spending is bad."

The problem with these statements is that they are incomplete. We live in a complex world, and these labels reduce our humanity and complex brainpower into something that's flat and incomplete. The reality is that sometimes government regulations are bad. Other times, government regulations are good. Sometimes businesses can do some really great things for society. Other times businesses can do some pretty nasty things. When we label something as good or bad, our minds become closed. We become attached to the position, and our brains will highlight to us evidence that supports our beliefs. For instance, if you believe Republicans are bad, you will notice more and more evidence to back up that opinion. If you believe Republicans are good, you will notice more and more evidence to back up that opinion as well. Pretty soon, we are not seeing the world as it is anymore. Instead, we only see what we already believe.

Oversimplification in our thinking is a danger that lifestyle business owners actively seek to avoid. Things are rarely always bad or always good. Our world is too complex for such simplified statements or beliefs. When we put a label on things, all we see is the label and nothing else. The military knows this well. By labeling people as either friendlies or enemies, the military makes it easier for soldiers to shoot somebody. If a soldier has to think beyond the labels and contemplate how the person he or she is shooting at may also be a human being with fears and hopes—a husband who loves his spouse, a father who loves his children, a person who likes spicy food, a person who likes to tell jokes, and a person who grew up in a different world than the soldier's—it would be a lot more difficult to pull the trigger on anyone, and the military wouldn't have order anymore. By giving the soldiers a label to go by, it effectively shuts down any higher-level thinking; all the soldier has to do is follow orders and pull the trigger on someone labeled as an enemy.

As a lifestyle business owner, you need to avoid oversimplification. Our world is complex, and you need all the higher-level thinking you can get. Labels can help us understand something, but remember that labels are flat and incomplete.

Principle 3: Value the process. We live in a society in which often the only thing that matters is whether or not you've achieved the goal. It doesn't matter how you get there. As long as you've achieved the goal, you are seen as a winner.

When we forget to value the process and focus solely on achievement, we can do some pretty destructive things along the way.

I know a lot of people in the business and tech community worship Steve Jobs. He is put on a pedestal and hailed as the ultimate sign of success. The 2015 film *Steve Jobs* gives a glimpse into how he treated those who worked with him. If you haven't seen the film, it can be an eye opener to see a side of Steve Jobs that most people don't know. Although the filmmakers likely exaggerated and dramatized many things to make the film interesting to watch, the depiction of Steve Jobs as a tyrant is not entirely without ground, based on the many biographies and profiles of the man. My question is, "Is it worth treating people poorly just to achieve your goal? Why can't you do both—treat people nicely and achieve your goal?"

In the business world, there is a popular belief that winning is the only thing that matters. It doesn't matter how you get there—if you have to lie, cheat, steal, pollute, or treat people poorly, so be it. As long as you achieve the goal (which is usually making a lot of money), people will see you as a winner. This line of thinking has led to many disasters in the past, such as General Electric dumping industrial waste directly into the Hudson River, Boeing greatly polluting the Duwamish River, and people still hailing GE and Boeing as highly admired companies because they make a lot of money. I am not saying GE and Boeing are good or bad. Doing so would be oversimplification. There are good sides and bad sides to these companies.

Lifestyle business owners pay just as much attention to achieving the goal as they do to how they get there. I've met business owners who make a lot of money, but their marriage is a mess and they hardly know their kids. Inwardly, I wonder, What's the point? Society may see them as a success because they run a successful business, but in my opinion, they have given up too much to get there. In fact, they were using an either/or mind-set. They didn't ask themselves how they could run a great business *and* have a great marriage *and* be an amazing parent. If you find yourself thinking, It's impossible to do all of the above, just remember that avoiding binary thinking forces your brain to engage in higher-level thinking, innovation, and creative solutions.

Paying attention to the process applies not only to how you live your life and how you run your business but also to how you conduct meetings. When I am in a meeting, I am paying just as much attention to the content as the process. Let's say we are in a meeting about budgets. The content is what people say about the budget. The process is how people say it, who is dominating the conversation and who is silent, whether there is trust in the room, whether people are saying what they really think or are just agreeing to please the boss, and so on. How well the group worked together is as much a sign of success as finishing the budget. Valuing the process is hard work and takes longer to get things done. It's much easier and quicker to shut someone up who doesn't agree with you or to not pay attention to who is not speaking his or her mind. You'll end up with a result that is inferior, though. You may have a decision, but there is a lack of buy-in and support from some people in the group. You may make progress in the short run but run into nasty side effects in the long run.

Lifestyle business owners believe that achieving the goal and how you get there both matter. Honor the process as much as you honor the destination.

Principle 4: Systemized assumption questioning. Have you ever wondered how three different witnesses can see the same car accident and tell three different stories of what happened? The reason is that we don't actually perceive reality. Our brain takes in as much information as it can, runs it through various filters of what to ignore and what to pay attention to, and builds a model in our mind of how the world works.

One of the most noticeable examples of the model in our mind not reflecting reality is when we travel to a foreign country and experience culture shock. What you believe to be appropriate attire may not be appropriate at all in another country. What you believe to be polite may actually be offensive. These are times when we realize the assumptions we have no longer hold true in that culture.

In *The 7 Habits of Highly Effective People,* Stephen Covey shares the story of one morning when he was riding the subway in New York. People were sitting quietly—some were reading newspapers, some were lost in thought, some had their eyes closed. Suddenly, a man walked onto the train with some very out-of-control children. The children were yelling, running around, and bothering other people on the subway. The most surprising thing was that the man didn't do anything and simply ignored it. Covey thought this man was very rude and finally decided to confront him, asking if he would please keep his children under control. The man lifted his gaze as if to come to a consciousness of the situation for the first time. He said softly, "Oh, you're right. I guess I should do something about it. We just came from the hospital, where their mother died about an hour ago. I don't know what to think, and I guess they don't know how to handle it either." All of a sudden, Covey's perspective changed. He went from feeling angry to feeling sympathetic.

Lifestyle business owners recognize that your thinking is only as good as the model you build in your mind. If the assumptions you hold are not accurate, the model in your head will also not accurately reflect the world. One of the most powerful tools that lifestyle business owners utilize is a systemized process to question their own assumptions. Whenever they feel stuck, they ask themselves, "What assumptions am I bringing to the situation? What do I assume to be true?" Once they consciously list their assumptions, they ask themselves, "Is this actually true?"

We make all sorts of assumptions in our daily lives. Here are some examples:

- "Anyone who cuts me off in traffic is a jerk." Is this actually true? Or could it be someone trying to drive a woman in labor to the hospital?
- "Anyone who drives too slowly can't drive." Is this actually true? Or could it be the driver in front of you sees a cop ahead?
- "My employees will run my business into the ground if I am not there on a daily basis." Is this actually true? Or is it your fear talking? Or is it the fact that you don't have systems and checks in place?

I invite you to question your assumptions the next time you feel stuck. Ask yourself, "What do I assume to be true? And is it actually true?" Noticing and questioning your own assumptions is humbling and requires letting go of your ego, but it is a habit that lifestyle business owners regularly practice to tackle their dilemmas.

Principle 5: Systemized reflection. Lifestyle business owners make it a practice to reflect at specific times. The following are some examples.

- At the end of every year, they ask themselves, "What worked well in my business this year? What did not work well in my business this year?"
- At the end of every month, they ask themselves, "What worked well in my business this month? What did not work well in my business this month?"
- At the end of every employee meeting, they ask themselves, "What worked well during the meeting today? What did not work well during the meeting today?"

In addition to reflecting on themselves, lifestyle business owners also invite their employees to reflect. At the end of every employee meeting, a lifestyle business owner invites everyone to talk about what worked well during the meeting and what didn't. You'll be surprised at what you hear when you invite people to share what worked for them and what didn't. Having this input is crucial to making the next meeting run better than this meeting did.

Believe it or not, your employees want to help you succeed. The more profitable your business is, the more you can afford to give out raises. I see many business owners whose employees are clueless as to whether the company is doing well or suffering. Imagine holding an employee meeting once a month and inviting everyone to talk about what worked well this month and what didn't work well. Encourage people to share what worked well and didn't work well for them personally as well as what's working well and not working well for the company.

Regular reflection is the key to continuous improvement. Regular group reflection allows new ideas to be shared, tried, and improved over time. During these reflection opportunities, it is important to pay attention to the group dynamics and make it a safe place for people to share what they really think. If people are holding back for fear of getting into trouble, meaningful reflection won't take place. As the business owner, you have a lot of power. If you talk a lot during these employee meetings, your employees will simply shut up and agree with you. I encourage business owners to talk less during these meetings and listen more. Ask a lot of questions, such as the following: How are things working for you? What do you think worked well for our business this month?

What didn't work so well for the company this month? What do you think is working well for our customers? What do you think is not working well for our customers? How is our work environment? What do you like about our work environment? What do you not like about our work environment? What did you think of the meeting today? What worked well for you? What didn't work well for you?

In *The E-Myth Revisited,* Michael Gerber encourages business owners to spend more time working *on* their business rather than working *in* their business. I agree with his message and encourage you to not only work *on* your business through regular personal reflection but also work *on* your business with your employees through regular group reflection. The more you reflect personally and invite your employees to reflect with you as a group on a regular basis, the more empowered your employees will feel, the more motivated they will be to work for you, the more solutions to tough challenges you will come up with as a group, and the more adaptable and resilient your business will be to a fast-changing world.

Seeing the Bigger Picture

In this chapter, I have covered the five principles in which lifestyle business owners think differently from ordinary business owners. One, lifestyle business owners avoid binary thinking. Two, they avoid oversimplification. Three, they value how the goal is achieved as much as they value the goal itself. Four, they regularly question their own assumptions. And five, they regularly engage in individual reflection as well as group reflection.

The best way to learn something is to practice it. Don't just read about these principles of thinking—put them into practice! I encourage you to go through these five principles of thinking and find a way to apply them in your life or your business. The more you practice these five principles of thinking, the more you will see the bigger picture, and the better decisions you will make.

~ INVITATION TO ACT ~

What is your biggest takeaway from this chapter?

_____

_____

_____

_____

_____

~ Free Training Videos ~
Visit www.LifestyleBusinessOwner.com
to download
your free training videos on
becoming a lifestyle business owner!

CHAPTER 14

Decide What Is Worth Pursuing

In the last chapter, I challenged you to think hard about the way you think. In this chapter, I want to challenge you to examine what is actually worth pursuing. The hallmark of lifestyle business owners is designing the business around their values, lifestyles, and priorities. I want you to think hard about what your priorities actually are. Only when you have a crystal clear idea of what you really want can you build a business centered around your priorities.

Some of the things I say in this chapter may make you feel uncomfortable. If you find yourself feeling uneasy about what I've said, please know that it is intentional and that I do it only in the interest of serving you. Some of the cultural messaging I am going to point out is so deep in people's subconscious and taken for granted by so many people that we simply don't take the time to examine whether we really agree with these assumptions.

In the business world, there is a very popular idea that the more money you make, the more valuable you are as a person. A CEO who makes $1 million a year is more successful than a midlevel employee who makes $70,000 a year. The midlevel employee who makes $70,000 a year is more successful than the janitor who makes minimum wage. The message here is that money equals success, and the more money you make, the more successful you are. A billionaire is more successful than a millionaire. As a culture, we look up to people who make a lot of money. We are fascinated by the list of the richest people in the world compiled every year by *Forbes* magazine. This cultural message assumes that the more money you make, the better off you are.

Another powerful cultural message is that growth is always good. If our economy grows, that is good. If our economy doesn't grow, our politicians panic and start devising all sorts of ways to bring our economy back to a growing phase. If you listen to the news, you will hear the assumption that if everything is working right, our economy should always be growing. I hear the same sort of logic when I speak with business owners. Most business owners are always asking me how they can grow their business. They want more sales. They want more profits. They want a bigger operation. They don't think about whether owning a bigger business will actually make them happier. They are operating under the assumption that growth equals success, so they pursue more and more growth without thinking about whether having more will actually improve their quality of life.

Becoming a lifestyle business owner means there are things that are more important to you than just money. Perhaps one of those things is free time. Perhaps one is having more meaning in your life. Perhaps one is having a lower amount of stress. Perhaps one is feeling a sense of contribution. Perhaps one is happiness. Perhaps one is quality of life. Contrary to the traditional paradigm that more money is always better and more growth is always better, lifestyle business owners take the time to decide for themselves what is really important to them.

I invite you to take some time to decide what is worth pursuing for you. To help you with this process, I'd like to share with you the Worthwhile Goals Framework:

Let's go through each of these three elements one at a time.

What Do You Really Want for You?

Every one of us has a unique reason for wanting to become a lifestyle business owner. What do you really want for you? Is it better health? Is it lower stress? Is it more time with your loved ones? Is it to feel a sense of contribution? Is it making more money, beating the competition, and growing the company?

None of these reasons are right or wrong. I invite you to be honest with yourself and not let our society or culture dictate what success really means to you. Many times you will find that multiple things are important to you. For instance, I have a friend who owns a marketing and administrative-support-service business, and here are the things he has decided are important to him:

- *Financial ability to live comfortably.* Notice he didn't say "making more money is always better." As long as the company makes enough for him to live comfortably, he is happy.

- *Environmental stewardship.* He cares a lot about the impact he and his company have on the environment. He estimates the amount of carbon emissions generated as a result of his company operations and sets aside corresponding company funds to purchase carbon offsets, making it a carbon-neutral company. He investigates carbon-offset companies carefully and chooses holistic solutions that not only help fight climate change but also help improve the local communities and economies. He pays a lot of attention to how much energy is wasted, how much paper is wasted, whether the workplace recycles and composts, whether the copier paper is 100 percent recycled, and so forth. To him, environmental stewardship is a measure of success that is just as important as the company's financial profitability.

- *Health and work-life balance.* Only working four days a week is another conscious choice he made to maintain his work-life balance. I am not talking about people who work "compressed workweeks" and end up working ten hours a day for four days a week—the equivalent of a typical forty-hour workweek. He takes Wednesdays off and works eight hours a day on the remaining days. At some point in the future, when the time is right, he may choose to rearrange his life and business to work even fewer hours.

- *Stress level.* Having a low-stress work environment is another measure of success for him. Some work environments are highly stressful, and he has made deliberate choices to choose work that doesn't stress him out. Having a manageable amount of stress is fine and even healthy, but he makes sure that his work life is not a highly stressful one.

- *Personal growth.* Another area that is important to him is whether he is growing as a person as a result of owning this business. Is he becoming the person he wants to become? He takes time at the end of every year to reflect on what kind of person he is becoming. Is he getting more arrogant? Or is he getting humbler? Is he getting harsher? Or is he getting kinder? Is he getting more assertive? Or is he getting more timid? Is he acknowledging the role of pure luck in his success? Or is he over his head and thinking that the success he has experienced is all due to his personal efforts? To own a successful business, he needs to grow as a person.

What my friend really wants may be very different from what you really want. His measures of business success may be very different from yours. What do you really want for you? It's easy to say, "I want more happiness," but I challenge you to be more specific. What are the conditions that will lead to your happiness?

What Do You Really Want for Your Employees?

Once you've given some thought about what you really want for yourself, I invite you to think about what you really want for your employees. Do you want them to feel financially secure about the state of the company? If so, do your employees know how the company is doing? Do you want your employees to love the place they work? If so, do you know how your employees really feel about their work environment? Do you want your employees to live a balanced life? Do you know how many hours your employees spend on their daily commute? Do you want your employees to grow as people as a result of being a part of your company? Do you want them to become more capable over time? How would you like them to grow? How would they like to grow? Do you want your employees to be healthy and full of vitality? Have you ever thought about what your employees eat for lunch? Do they even eat lunch? Do they work through lunch? Do they take breaks throughout the day? Do they burn out? Are they stressed to the max? Do you want your employees to feel valued by their supervisors and coworkers?

Lifestyle business owners take the time to write down what they really want for their employees. Gone are the days when a business owner could offer just a paycheck and nothing more. To attract and retain the best talent, the business owner needs to care about the well-being of his or her employees. Caring about the well-being of your employees doesn't necessarily mean you need to offer the most comprehensive benefits. There is a big difference between throwing a benefits package at someone and being a business owner who genuinely cares. I know plenty of disempowered and unhappy employees who work at companies that offer great benefit packages such as excellent health insurance, 401(k) accounts, and life insurance. Employees can feel it when the business is a heartless machine that doesn't really care. As a business owner, your genuine desire to care for your employees' well-being often means more than the types of benefits you can actually offer. You may be surprised to learn that many business owners don't really care about their employees. They see their employees as replaceable parts, and the well-being of their employees matters very little as long as the business makes a lot of money for the owners. I invite you to be honest with yourself and write down what you really want for your employees.

What Do You Really Want for Your Company?

Now that you've thought about what you really want for yourself and what you really want for your employees, the next step is to write down what you really want for your company. Do you want your company to be a leader in terms of profitability? Do you want your company to be a leader in environmental stewardship? Do you want your company to do good for society through its very operations?

What do you want your company to represent? Let's say you own a manufacturing company that produces hazardous waste. Although there are laws on the disposal of hazardous waste, the laws aren't as strict as they could be, and the government agencies aren't always watching. Does your company do only the minimum? Does your company follow the rules only when someone is watching? Does your company change its behavior only when it is forced to by regulations? Or do you want your company to voluntarily do more good for society than what is required?

What kind of company culture do you want to foster? When it comes to workplace culture, actions speak louder than words. Many companies say they put their people first, but their actions show the opposite. Many companies may advertise that they are green, but they do only the minimum, cutting corners when no one is watching or cutting corners on a certain job if the customer doesn't particularly care about being green. If integrity is a value you want to foster, you've got to model by example.

As you reflect on what you really want for your company, you may be tempted by binary thinking. Some people say to me, "Aaron, I can't run a profitable business *and* do all these other things such as being green, not cutting corners, and being nice to my employees." If you find yourself thinking this way, ask yourself what assumptions you are bringing to the situation, and ask yourself whether these assumptions are actually true. It's easy to fall into binary thinking: "I can either have this or have that." It's hard work to innovate and come up with creative ways for how you can have both.

I want to share with you some innovations that exemplify the way lifestyle business owners think. In a fast-changing world, a company that is not resilient will likely go out of business. In their book *Prosper!: How to Prepare for the Future and Create a World Worth Inheriting*, Chris Martenson and Adam Taggart talk about eight ways to improve one's resilience. They call them the eight forms of capital. I invite you to think about how you can build these eight forms of capital in your business to increase its resilience.

1. *Financial capital.* Most people think about money when they hear the word *capital*. This is capital in the most traditional sense. Is your company profitable? Are your company funds well managed? Do you have the proper financial reserves to weather the bad times?

2. *Living capital.* Living capital refers to things that are alive. You are alive—are you valuing your health? Your employees are alive—are you valuing their well-being and vitality? Nature is alive—is your business killing nature or helping to keep nature alive?

3. *Material capital.* Material capital refers to the physical tools your company utilizes. Perhaps your computers, printers, and credit-card machines are so slow that it is worth upgrading them to increase your productivity. Perhaps you switch out the old toilet for a water-saving toilet that saves a lot of water and reduces your monthly water bill.

4. *Knowledge capital.* Knowledge is a very powerful form of capital. Whenever a key employee leaves your company, how much knowledge is lost? Are you taking advantage of the knowledge that actually exists within your company? Do you encourage your employees to share their knowledge? Do you encourage the cross-pollination of ideas—meaning

you encourage your employees to build on each other's ideas instead of shutting down a new idea that is not completely well formed yet?

5. *Emotional capital.* How well do you handle business failures and setbacks? If something is not going well with your business, do you fall apart emotionally? How well do you and your employees behave when things get stressful? How well do you and your employees communicate with the customers and vendors when both sides are upset? How well do you handle sensitive conversation topics with your employees?

6. *Social capital.* The relationships that are built between you and your employees, the relationships between your employees and each other, the relationships between your business and its customers, and the relationships between your business and its vendors are all examples of social capital. Have you ever heard the saying that it's not what you know but who you know? Social relationships are valuable. How well do your people know each other? How well do they know the customers? How well does the team function? Is the team dysfunctional, or is there synergy occurring?

7. *Cultural capital.* Company culture is an important concern for business owners. Having a toxic work environment is probably the number one reason good employees quit. Your company culture is the unspoken rules of acceptable behavior at the workplace. Is it okay to really speak your mind? Is being five minutes late acceptable in practice? Do employees need to kiss up to the boss to get promoted? Is the company's commitment to being green just on the surface, because it's what customers want to hear, or does the company actually care about environmental stewardship? Does the boss actually care about the well-being of the employees, or does he just say empty words? At every company, there is a set of spoken and written rules and a set of unspoken and unwritten rules. When it comes to behavior, people will follow the unspoken and unwritten rules. Pay special attention to how these unspoken and unwritten rules shape your company's culture, because they drive people's behavior no matter who you hire.

8. *Time capital.* Small businesses are more nimble than large corporations are. As a small-business owner, you can take advantage of your speed and adapt to changing market conditions quickly if you have been paying attention to the market. Time is an ever-depleting resource. Are you putting your time to its best use? Are your employees putting their time to the best possible use? How people spend their time can be a reflection of what they truly value. If you value building wealth, how much time do you spend working on building your wealth? If you value sustainability, how much time do you spend working on becoming more sustainable? If you spend several hours a day watching TV, what does that say about what you truly value?

Thinking about how you can develop these eight forms of capital will help you and your business become more resilient over time. Resilience building is one example of social innovation that exemplifies how lifestyle business owners think. Yes, building financial resilience is important, but financial capital is only one of the eight forms of capital. How can you build or maximize all eight forms of capital?

Let me share with you another innovation that falls right in line with the way lifestyle business owners think. In the traditional business world, making profits is the only thing that matters. If the government wants to pass a regulation that requires power companies to reduce the amount of harmful emissions they emit into the air, you can pretty much count on the power companies hiring attorneys to fight this regulation in court. After all, having to upgrade their plant to emit less harmful stuff will hurt their profits—at least in the short-run. Many business owners have thought hard about this paradigm of seeing profits as the only thing that matters and have begun to question whether we are doing the right thing when we measure our success solely based on the bottom line.

The innovation is to create more than one bottom line. Right now, there is only one bottom line: profits. More and more business owners are asking, "Why can't my company have more than one bottom line?" In fact, some business owners have done so. There are businesses that have three bottom lines. The first bottom line is profit, which is still important because a company that is unprofitable cannot exist in the long-term. The second bottom line is environmental impact. What is the impact of the company on our environment? Is the company harming the environment through its operations or making the environment better? The third bottom line is social impact. What is the impact of the company on our society? Is the company making the local community stronger? Is the company treating its employees well? The term for businesses like this is *triple bottom line*. These businesses manage for environmental impact and social impact as much as they manage for financial profitability. It's like having three different subjects to excel at. Think of a high-school student who studies math, English, and history. Let's say the student gets an A in math but gets a D in English and an F in history. Would you consider the student successful? Well, imagine your business is taking three subjects and being graded by three teachers. How well is it doing financially? How well is it doing environmentally? And how well is it doing socially? Would you consider your business successful if it gets an A in one area but fails the other two?

Food for thought. What do you really want for your company?

The Western Obsession to Measure Things

In Western cultures, people place a high value on things they can measure. There is a popular belief that you can only manage what you can measure. If you can't measure it, it's not important. Taken to the extreme, this management philosophy becomes something like "if you can't measure it, it doesn't exist."

I want to challenge you to do better than that. It may be hard to measure the well-being of your employees, but does that mean it's unimportant? It may be hard to measure the impact of your business on the environment, but does that mean it's unimportant? It may be hard to measure the impact of your business on the local community, but does that mean it's unimportant?

I challenge you to decide what's important to you. It may be a list of four things, or it may be a list of six things. If the well-being of your employees is one of the areas that is important to you, I also challenge you to find out what's important to your employees from their perspective. Once you have made a complete list of all the areas that are worth pursuing, go through each one and ask yourself the following questions:

- What can be quantitatively measured?
- What can be qualitatively measured?
- What can't be measured but is important nonetheless?

At the end of every year, I invite you to write an annual report on the state of your company. You don't have to share it with anyone else. This letter is more for you than it is for anyone else. In a publicly traded company, the CEO would write a letter to the shareholders describing the state of the company. Since you are the shareholder of your own business, I invite you to write a letter to yourself describing the state of your company.

In this letter, I want you to talk about how your company is doing in each of the areas that you've decided are worth pursuing. Let's say you've decided to use the triple-bottom-line model. In this case, you would write about whether your company was successful financially this year, whether your company was successful environmentally this year, and whether your company was successful socially this year. In other words, how are we doing in the areas that matter? Financially, how are our sales doing? How are our profits doing? Environmentally, how are we doing? Is the company hurting nature or protecting nature through its operations? Socially, how are we doing? Are you, the business owner, happy with your lifestyle? Are your employees happy with their jobs? Is the business contributing to society or taking things away?

If you feel brave, you can share this letter with your employees, but you don't have to. There are benefits to sharing this letter with your employees. At most companies, the employees are kept in the dark. They have no idea whether the company is doing well or not. With limited information, they may repeatedly ask for raises, not knowing that the company is in financial trouble. Sharing this letter with your employees can also lead to higher employee satisfaction. Part of the satisfaction of working hard is knowing how well the team has performed. If the team has worked hard to increase revenues, wouldn't it make them feel good to see the results? If the team has worked hard to save paper and recycle more, wouldn't it make them feel good to know how well they've done? Whether people are employees or business owners, they are still human beings. As human beings, we want meaning in our lives, and we seek opportunities where we have a chance to make a difference and be a part of something that is bigger than ourselves. Why not turn your business into a place where the employees feel they are actively making a difference?

Sometimes business owners ask me, "Aaron, I understand that just because something is hard to measure doesn't mean it's not worth pursuing. But how do I manage for the things that are really hard to measure? For instance, I want my employees to feel happy coming to work, but how am I supposed to control their happiness?" That is a very good question. And the answer is that you can't control someone's happiness, but you can often control the conditions that encourage happiness to occur more often. Have you ever been to a grocery store where the clerk at the checkout counter looks completely bored? If I had to stand at the same place and scan groceries for my entire eight-hour shift, I would probably get bored too. But I was at a grocery store recently where all the clerks at the checkout counter were full of life and vitality. They were having animated conversations with the customers, you could see the smiles on their faces, and they seemed to be really enjoying their jobs. I couldn't help but wonder, *What is this grocery store doing differently?* When I asked the clerk about this, she said to me, "One of the nice things about working here is that you get to do every job in the store during each shift. No one is ever checking out groceries for eight hours straight. You switch between stocking shelves, helping customers, checking out groceries, and working in the back, so you never get bored."

I thought to myself, *What a great idea! This grocery store is not necessarily paying higher wages, but someone cared about employee happiness.* As you list the areas that are important for you to pursue, you will find that some things are harder to measure than others. In many cases, there is no universal standard to measure the social impact or the environmental impact of your business. But don't let that stop you. Sometimes all it takes is for someone to care.

~ INVITATION TO ACT ~
What is your biggest takeaway from this chapter?

_____

_____

_____

_____

_____

_____

~ Free Training Videos ~
Visit www.LifestyleBusinessOwner.com
to download
your free training videos on
becoming a lifestyle business owner!

CHAPTER 15

Becoming the Background Leader

As you work toward becoming a lifestyle business owner, you may find yourself wanting to work fewer hours than you do now. Don't get me wrong. You can be a lifestyle business owner working forty hours a week if that's the lifestyle you want to live, but many business owners I meet would prefer to work fewer hours than that. Not being at your business all the time implies that you need to lead from the background instead of leading from the foreground. In this chapter, I want to engage in a dialogue with you about leadership and how lifestyle business owners are as leaders.

What comes to your mind when you think of the image of a great leader? Do you think of someone who is confident? Someone who knows the answers and tells people what to do? If I were to make a pose with my body to represent a leader, do you picture me making a "Hercules pose"—raising my arms, flexing my muscles, and smiling confidently?

The Chinese philosopher Lao Tzu has a different idea of what a great leader looks like. He says, "A leader is best when people barely know he exists. When his work is done, his aim fulfilled, they will say: 'We did it ourselves.'" In other words, Lao Tzu is saying that the best leaders are invisible. They are not confidently leading on the front lines and telling people what to do. In fact, the best leaders want people to feel like *they did it themselves,* so that after the leader is gone, people will continue to work together and make things happen.

I am contrasting two styles of leadership here. The traditional style of leadership is one of a commander. The commander is highly visible and confident and tells people what to do because the commander knows best and always has the answers. The second style of leadership is one of the background leader. Background leaders work in the background and are primarily invisible. They don't have all the answers, and, frankly, they don't need to. The focus of background leaders is to foster an environment that empowers people to work together. The commander's aim is to be in power and be there all the time with the answers. After all, people look up to the commander and wait for the commander to tell them what to do next. In contrast, the aim of the background leader is to fade into the background as soon as appropriate. Initially, the background leader may take a more prominent role to get people to come together and develop a shared vision. But the background leader doesn't want people to depend on him or her for instructions. The background leader empowers people to make decisions and observes how things go from a distance. If people on the team work well together, the background leader stays in the background. If people on the team get into conflict and cannot function together, the background leader steps in to help people work it out and steps back into the background as soon as appropriate.

There are several reasons that the background style of leadership is more appropriate for lifestyle business owners. First, if you employ the commander style of leadership, your employees will always be looking to you to tell them what to do, and you will have a hard time taking off and enjoying more free time in your life. Second, you will be more likely to build employee goodwill and retain your good employees long-term by employing the background style of leadership. The reason is that people work best when they feel alive and empowered. Think about it. Would you prefer a boss who values your input and asks how you can design a work environment together that makes everyone who works at the business feel excited to come to work every day? Or would you prefer a military-style commander as a boss—one who gives orders and expects you to follow them without question? In many companies, employees learn to keep their mouths shut because contradicting the ideas of their superiors is equivalent to losing their jobs or kissing their potential promotion good-bye. What kind of work environment do you think the top talents choose to work in? Last but not least, employing the background style of leadership will make your company more profitable, innovative, and resilient. We no longer live in an age in which one person knows all the answers. Our world has become increasingly interconnected and complex, and you cannot expect one person, no matter how smart, to hold all the answers to all the challenges your business will ever face. Lifestyle business owners know that one of the greatest assets of their business is the people they hire. By employing the background style of leadership, the lifestyle business owner taps into the ideas and unique perspectives of each person and gets everyone to work together toward a shared vision. In turn, the company is more adaptable and resilient to business challenges, because you have a team of smart people working out the best way to solve something instead of being dependent on an all-knowing leader for the answers to all possible business challenges.

Examine Your Assumptions

To make the change from commander-style leadership to background-style leadership, start by examining your assumptions. What are your assumptions when it comes to your employees? Do you believe that your employees are dumb? Do you believe that they are smart? Do you believe that your employees can come up with a solution to a business problem that you can't come up with? Or do you believe that if you can't figure something out, none of your employees can?

What are your assumptions when it comes to your role as the business owner? Do you believe it is your job to come up with the solution and tell everyone what to do? Do you believe you need to know all the answers in order to be respected as a leader? Or do you believe that it is your job to foster an environment that allows people to work together and figure out as a team the best way to tackle a business challenge?

What are your assumptions when it comes to the role of your employees? Are you looking for minions who will follow your system without question?

Or are you looking for people who will follow the procedures of the company *and* provide valuable input as to how the procedures of the company could be improved?

What are your assumptions when it comes to differences? Do you believe that the ideal situation is one in which everyone agrees with you? Or do you believe that ideas different from yours are valuable and that diversity in ideas is something to be fostered?

What are your assumptions when it comes to this book? Do you believe I am naive and idealistic and my advice would never work in your situation? Do you believe there is only one right way to run a business? Or do you believe there are multiple right ways to run a business?

Notice the Power Dynamics

If you have been running your company using the commander-style leadership, your employees will not suddenly feel empowered and come forth with all sorts of ideas that might be different from yours. The traditional business world is filled with commander-style leaders, and employees are trained to keep quiet whenever they have an opinion different from their boss's. Whenever the employees notice something wrong or feel mistreated by the company, they must constantly weigh their need for income against the risks of bringing it up and potentially losing their jobs or being perceived negatively by their superiors and therefore being passed over for promotion opportunities.

Before anyone on your team will openly collaborate with you and with each other, everyone needs to feel safe. If the threat of losing one's job or being passed over for raises is constantly looming, no one will openly share what he or she really thinks. As the owner of the business, you have a lot of power. You have the power to fire people and either give or deny raises. The relationship between you and your employees is far from one in which each side has equal power. In fact, you hold almost all the power. If you do not pay attention to how your power comes across, your employees will simply tell you what you want to hear.

Recognizing the power dynamics at play is key to being an effective background leader. There are three types of power. Let's start with the easiest one to see: *authority power*. Authority power is power by decree. To find out whether someone has authority power, just look at the person's title and where this person fits in the organization chart (or "food chain," so to speak). For instance, perhaps your manager has the authority to oversee the other employees but not the authority to hand out raises. A person's power of authority is clearly stated. If you lead people using your authority power alone (that is, "I am your boss, so you need to do what I say"), people may be forced to follow you, but whether they do it willingly is another matter.

The second type of power is called *agenda power*—the ability to influence the agenda. The person with agenda power may or may not be the same as the person with authority power. Have you ever experienced a situation in your life in which the person with the title is technically in charge, but if you truly want to get something done, you need to go to someone else? The person with agenda power has the influence to make things happen or change the direction of the agenda. Here's an example to illustrate the difference between authority power and agenda power. Suppose you are a parent and you are trying to convince your teenage daughter to make a particular choice. As the parent, you have the authority power. You can ground her or make her life miserable in some other way if she doesn't listen to you, but forcing her to do what you want using your authority doesn't always produce the desired result. Sometimes it pays to figure out who has the agenda power with your daughter. Maybe it's her best friend. If you can convince her best friend to talk to your daughter, her best friend might be a much greater influence on your daughter than you are. Do you see the distinction here? The person with the title is not necessarily the person with the influence to get things done. If you want to create change, you need to pay attention not only to who has the authority power but also to who has the agenda power.

The third form of power is the most powerful of the three, but it is also the hardest to see. It is called *culture power*. The reason it is hard to see is that no single person possesses it. It is like air. It is all around you, but if you don't pay attention to it, you won't even notice it. Every company has a culture. Every family has a culture. Every city or town has a culture. The culture of a place is a set of unspoken, unwritten rules for acceptable social behavior. No one questions why it's done this way, because "this is just the way things are done around here."

Some companies have a workaholic culture. There is no company rulebook that says everyone has to work fourteen-hour days and not take weekends off, but that's what everybody does. If you don't belong in this culture, you leave. Other companies have a don't-question-your-superiors culture. In these companies, the power distance between each level of the organization is huge. If your boss says something, you better follow it. If an idea comes from your boss's boss, you better make it your top priority. And if the idea comes from your boss's boss's boss, you better treat it like the word of God. Culture power is the greatest form of power because it influences us without us realizing it. Leaders come and go, but the culture tends to stay. Think about your city. Elected officials (ones with authority power) come and go, but the culture of the city tends to stay the same.

Background leaders are acutely aware of the power dynamics at play in a company. As the owner of the business, you are clearly at the top of the food chain when it comes to authority power. You may or may not be the person holding the agenda power. Yet culture power doesn't reside just in you. It resides in everyone. Everyone has agreed nonverbally that these are the acceptable social behaviors at this company. Think about the influence of company culture for a moment. What are the unspoken, unwritten rules for acceptable social behavior at your company? What sorts of behaviors result in a slap on the wrist and what sorts of behaviors don't? Is it okay to openly say you think the boss's idea is stupid? Are certain employees treated like gold while others are treated like dirt? Is arriving a little late socially acceptable? Is it socially expected to check your work e-mail on vacation? What unspoken message is being sent when an employee sends the boss an e-mail at 11:15 p.m. and receives a reply from the boss at 11:17 p.m.? One employee once said confidentially that her organization had a culture in which physical appearance was highly valued. If she did not wear enough makeup or show up to work with fashionable clothing, she would get looks from people and remarks on her clothes that were presented as jokes but were not really jokes. As a result of the social pressure, she felt forced to spend a lot of money buying a new wardrobe and extra time getting ready every day just to be able to work at this organization. She was an excellent employee but felt frustrated by the culture of her organization.

Establish Emotional Safety

In the examples above, imagine how much courage it would take for the female employee to share how frustrated she is by the social pressure she receives from her coworkers to dress up, an employee to point out that all the people getting promoted are workaholics, or an employee to point out the unspoken fact that certain people receive preferential treatment from those in charge. An honest conversation about the good, the bad, and the ugly of your company's culture is not easy, but it is absolutely necessary if you want to create a healthy work environment.

Just because your employees may feel a sense of job security (meaning they don't expect to be fired anytime soon) doesn't necessarily mean they feel emotionally safe to fully contribute their thoughts and ideas. To build a company that doesn't depend on you being the commander, you need to cultivate a culture of openness and collaboration. To do that, you need to establish a level of emotional safety so that every employee feels safe to truly voice what is on his or her mind.

When you are starting, it is important to be frank with your intentions so that your employees don't feel like you've read a self-help book and are now using the latest techniques you've learned on them. You need to share with your team why you are doing this. Perhaps you envision yourself being more hands-off over time, and you want to pass more responsibilities on to your team. Perhaps you've been a commander all this time, and you want to shift toward a company culture that depends less on you. Perhaps you care deeply about your employees' well-being and you want to work together with them to design a work environment in which everyone feels jazzed to come to work every day.

Since you have the authority as the owner of the company, you need to stress that no one is going to get in trouble as a result of what they've shared in these conversations. Sometimes prefacing the discussion by stating your intentions honestly and saying that no one will get in trouble are still not enough. People will test whether they are really safe by sharing something that is a tiny bit risky. If what they've shared is met by immediate resistance, people will get the unspoken message that they are not really safe to share anything risky.

The role of the background leader is to pay attention to the content as well as the context of the conversation. The content is the words people say, and the context is how everyone is feeling. Do you sense a feeling of safety in the room? Do you sense hostility? Or do you sense uncertainty or uneasiness in the air? Remember that no meaningful conversation can take place without everyone in the room feeling safe. A few individuals may dominate the conversation, but those feeling unsafe may silently go along just to get through this company meeting.

Hold a Company-Improvement Workshop

Some business owners find it extremely helpful to close the business for one day and require all the employees to attend a company-improvement workshop. The workshop is held at a location other than the business premises so that the phone is not ringing off the hook and the meaningful conversations are not interrupted by customers walking in. The reason I recommend closing the business for a day to hold the workshop instead of holding it on a weekend when your business is normally closed, let's say, is the unspoken message you are sending. Do you value your employees' time off? Do you value their work-life balance and the time they spend with their loved ones? Or do you require them to give up their weekend just to put company business first? Yes, you will miss out on some sales by closing your business for a day, but the returns are well worth it. I also believe every employee should attend this company-improvement workshop (instead of just senior management) because every person has something valuable to say about how the company can be improved. Think about the unspoken message you are sending to the lowly workers when you invite only senior management to brainstorm how the company should be improved. Who is valued enough to have a voice, and who is not?

Prior to the workshop, you may want to work with a professional workshop facilitator to determine the goals of the workshop and to design activities and conversation topics that will lead the group toward those goals. Perhaps the goal is to design a work environment in which everyone feels excited to come to work every day. Such a goal might involve honest and open conversations about the current company culture, what is not working for each person, and how the team can collaborate to improve the work environment for everyone. Perhaps the goal is to come up with solutions to the challenges the company is facing. Perhaps the goal is to increase the efficiency of company operations or to improve the environmental and social contribution of the company. Whatever the goal is, the workshop itself will be led by the professional facilitator. The business owner might introduce the facilitator at the beginning and share how important everyone's full participation is to the future of the company, but for the rest of the workshop, the business owner is simply a participant like everyone else is.

Although you can lead such a company-improvement workshop yourself, I recommend hiring a professional workshop facilitator for several reasons. First, the business owner is too entrenched personally in the business. If something that is said during the workshop causes the business owner to become defensive, all emotional safety disappears because the employees are now worried about getting fired. Second, the business owner is not always trained to handle hot, emotional topics in a way that makes everyone feel safe. Without the training and experience of a professional workshop facilitator, the difficult conversations might blow up. Finally, having someone else lead the workshop allows the business owner to be a participant just like everyone else is. Now that I've talked a lot about power dynamics, you may notice that having the business owner be a participant is an intentional move, because it sends the unspoken message that "I am in the same boat as you are, trying to work this out together with you" instead of "I've gathered you here to come up with something to my satisfaction." What's more, your goal is to become more of an invisible leader in the background and less of a commander-in-chief in the foreground.

The success of your company-improvement workshop depends on the extent to which people are willing to openly share their thoughts and ideas. To create an environment that encourages open collaboration, all efforts must be made to reduce the power distance between the superiors and subordinates. The message you want to send is this: "Today, we are all equals. Your ideas are just as valid as mine. I want to hear your ideas, and other people in the room want to hear your thoughts."

There are many things that can be done to reduce the power distance. Instead of arranging the tables and chairs in classroom style in which the person standing in front of the room is the authority figure, arrange them in a circle so that everyone is equal. Actually, get rid of the tables altogether—tables are barriers between people. Having people sit in chairs in a circle encourages the sharing of ideas.

At the start of your company-improvement workshop, I suggest the workshop facilitator invite people to introduce themselves in a very specific manner. We don't want people to bring up their title at the company, because it sets the tone that some people's ideas are worth more than others. Imagine if one person says, "My name is Bob Jones, and I am the president of the company." And the next person says, "My name is Joanne Williams, and I am a line worker." Right off the bat, we are setting people apart. Instead, I recommend people use only first names and not bring up their titles at all.

One way for the facilitator to accomplish this is to ask people to go around the room and share their first name, what they enjoy doing in their spare time, and their thoughts on the following question: "What do we need to do today to create an environment that is safe and comfortable for everyone to fully participate in?" It's a good idea to forego people's last names and titles because it reduces the power distance. Use first names only even if people already know each other, because the facilitator is new to the group. Asking people to share what they enjoy doing in their spare time gives everyone a chance to know each other a little better beyond the typical work environment. For instance, people may be surprised to learn that Joanne enjoys skydiving. We are nurturing an environment for meaningful dialogue to take place, and part of creating that environment is helping people know each other on a more personal level. Finally, the facilitator gives everyone the opportunity to voice their ideas on what needs to be done today in order to create an environment that is safe and comfortable for everyone to fully participate in. As each person shares his or her ideas, the facilitator writes them down on a large piece of paper that everyone can see. Once everyone in the room has shared, the facilitator can introduce himself or herself, share his or her hobby, and insert any other ground rules that would be helpful. For instance, one of the ground rules that is often helpful is for the group to build on each other's half-formed ideas instead of shooting them down because they have holes. Another ground rule might be for everyone to pay attention to the pacing of the conversation and how much pause there is between sentences, because some people are not comfortable interrupting and talking over others and may never get a chance to speak if the more dominant talkers do not leave enough pause for others to enter the conversation. Once all the ground rules have been written, the facilitator should ask the group if everyone is willing to abide by these rules for the duration of the workshop. Once a commitment is achieved, the facilitator can post this large piece of paper on the wall and hold participants accountable to these ground rules.

Design a Shared Vision

One of the topics I highly recommend people incorporate into their company-improvement workshop is designing a shared vision of the company. This is a time for people to openly talk about where the company was, where the company is today, and where they would like to see the company go in the future. In the previous chapter, I invited you to think about the areas that are worth pursuing. Imagine if all your employees were given a voice to talk about where they would like to see the company go.

The idea of developing a shared vision is about giving everyone a chance to talk about what is important to him or her when it comes to the workplace and the direction in which the company is heading. If you have a vision to pursue multiple bottom lines, this is a wonderful opportunity to share your ideas and get feedback from your employees. It's not about you dominating the conversation, and it's not about your employees making decisions for you. You still own the company, and you have the final say. But you value your employees' voices enough that you don't just make decisions without their input. You create a safe conversational environment that is away from the day-to-day busyness of your business. You listen to the wisdom in the room. You encourage people to build on each other's half-formed ideas instead of critiquing or shutting them down. Pretty soon, one idea leads to another, and you will find yourself immersed in a full-blown, meaningful dialogue designing the future of the company.

Bring the Unspoken Rules of Acceptable Social Behaviors Out into the Open

Another topic that I recommend people incorporate into their company-improvement workshop is a discussion on the unspoken rules of acceptable social behaviors at the company. Speaking openly about the company culture gives people a chance to examine what about the company culture is working for them and what is not.

As you can see, these can be sensitive topics. In order to create meaningful dialogue, there must be emotional safety in the room. That's why having firm ground rules at the beginning is so important. That's why having a facilitator trained to diffuse people who are upset can be really helpful. This is also a chance for you to be honest with yourself. Do you really want to become a background leader? Do you really want to improve your company? If so, are you open to hearing what your employees really think of their work environment? Are you willing to humble yourself and work with your employees to design something better? Are you willing to let go of the temptation to be the commander-in-chief, simply telling everyone how you want things to go and what you want people to do?

Hold a Dialogue on Team Dynamics

The company-improvement workshop is also a good place to hold a dialogue with the group about how well the group functions in the workplace. How about inviting each person to write down on a piece of paper—anonymously—how well he or she thinks the group functions together on a scale of one to ten (one being "we are a completely dysfunctional team at work" and ten being "we love working with each other and create lots of synergy by working together")? Have the facilitator collect everyone's ratings and read them out loud, and use these numbers as a point of discussion about how the team can better function together.

Throughout this whole process, your job is not to be the foreground leader and fix problems for people. You are there to be a background leader, to listen and offer ideas when appropriate. The intention is to train your people to resolve issues without needing you. The more you step in, the more dependent people will be on you. Your goal is to be in the background as much as possible, to pay attention to the level of emotional safety in the room, to notice if certain people are dominating the conversation while others are not getting a chance to talk, to ask good questions, and to ensure that every person has a chance to feel heard.

How to Start and End the Day

The facilitator should go through a check-in process at the beginning of the day and a check-out process at the end of the day. There are three objectives for the check-in process: to invite people to be mentally and emotionally present for the meeting, to help the participants know each other better, and to create an environment that is safe and comfortable for people to fully participate in. Notice that at the start of the day, I suggest having people sit in a circle and share their first name, hobby, and desired ground rules for emotional safety. This is one way to check in. The exact method of checking in will depend on the context of the meeting. If you are running a meeting on budgets, the check-in could be asking people to go around the room and share something about their day that would help them become present for the meeting and what they would like to accomplish during the meeting. I know it takes time to go through the check-in process, but it is definitely not time wasted. If people are not mentally present for the meeting and are still thinking about their day—if they do not have emotional safety or a clear intention of what they want to accomplish during the meeting—it will be difficult for meaningful dialogue to take place, and the meeting will likely get nowhere.

At the end of the day at your company-improvement workshop, I suggest the facilitator lead a check-out process, for which there are also three objectives: to find out what is working well, to find out what is not working well, and to gain commitment on the actions participants will take between now and the next time the group meets. One way to do this is for the facilitator to arrange the chairs in a circle and ask people to go around the room and share what worked well for them today and what did not work well. After everyone has shared, the facilitator can invite the group to discuss how things could be improved in the future. Finally, the meeting leader can invite the group to talk about what actions should be taken between now and the next meeting. It takes time to go through the check-out process, but like the check-in process, it is not time wasted. The check-out process is an opportunity for the group to reflect and improve. Remember systemized reflection? We are putting systems in place so that at the beginning of every meeting, your people go through the check-in process to maximize the effectiveness of the meeting. At the end of every meeting, your people reflect on how it went and how the next one could be made better. By teaching your people to check in and check out every time, you will empower them to create an environment that allows them to work better together over time.

Empower Your Team to Carry On without You

A successful company-improvement workshop is transformative. The business owner's paradigms are often transformed, and so are the employees.' A company's culture can also be shifted in a direction that supports more empowered employees and a business owner who fades more into the background. Each company-improvement workshop you hold is a chance for your team to bond more closely, talk about issues that matter to them, discuss how they can work better as a team, engage in dialogue with the owner on the company's current challenges and opportunities, and discuss where the team would like to see the company go in the future. People commit to what they help create. As you become a background leader and lifestyle business owner, your job is less and less about giving out orders for where you want your company to go and more and more about cocreating the future of your company with your staff.

How often should you hold these company-improvement workshops? It depends on your particular situation. After your first company-improvement workshop, which will take a full day, you can reflect on how things went and decide how often you want to hold future workshops. Some people like the idea of holding shorter (one hour or so) company-improvement meetings once a week, slightly longer (half-day) company-improvement meetings once a quarter, and a full-blown (one-day) company-improvement workshop once a year. You can hold the shorter company-improvement workshops on your own or even teach your staff how to hold them and let them lead the meeting, but I would definitely suggest having a professional facilitator lead the full-blown, one-day annual company-improvement workshops. I know everyone is busy, and it can seem like a waste of time to take people away from the day-to-day operations of your business to reflect and hold meaningful dialogues about how things can be improved. But trust me—this is not a waste of time. Your company operations will improve, your people will work better together, and your customers will receive superior service. With the proper design, you will also get to step more and more into the background, have an empowered team of people working toward goals and values that are important to the group, and experience the satisfaction and joy of being a lifestyle business owner.

~ INVITATION TO ACT ~
What is your biggest takeaway from this chapter?

_____

_____

_____

_____

_____

_____

~ Free Training Videos ~
Visit www.LifestyleBusinessOwner.com
to download
your free training videos on
becoming a lifestyle business owner!

Join the Wave

I invite you to join the wave of lifestyle business ownership. More and more people of all backgrounds and ages have started on the path to becoming lifestyle business owners. Owning a lifestyle business is possible for you. Yes, there are things that will be challenging for you, just as there are things that are difficult for me. I am not a natural public speaker, and I get extremely nervous every time I step in front of a camera, but I make videos that teach people how to become lifestyle business owners anyway—because I believe in you.

I don't know about you, but sometimes it can be pretty depressing to watch the news. The rich are getting richer and the poor are getting poorer. Big corporations are posting record profits, influencing politicians with powerful lobbyists, and evading taxes legally, while small businesses are struggling to survive. I want to live in a world that is thriving with small businesses. I want to live in a world in which it's desirable to be a small-business owner. Being a small-business owner should not mean you struggle with lack of profits, lack of time, or the stresses of having employees. Instead, being a small-business owner should mean living a great lifestyle, having plenty of free time, and making a difference through the very way you operate your business.

I have been fortunate enough to figure out how to systematically become a lifestyle business owner through decades in the school of hard knocks. I am still learning every day, but I have a pretty good sense of what works and what doesn't in the real world. Becoming a lifestyle business owner doesn't have to be a mystery. The process takes only three steps. Step one, buy a good business. Step two, increase your profits. Step three, empower your people. This is not the only way to become a lifestyle business owner, but it is the fastest and most consistent way to do so.

Now that you've read this book, where do you start? The first step to take is to look at where you are and decide where you want to go. If you don't have a business yet, perhaps a good goal is to meet with a business broker and look into buying a business. If you already have a business, you need to decide whether it is the right business for you. Just because a business was right for you in the past doesn't mean it is right for you now. Do you still enjoy owning this business? How does the future of the business look in light of what is happening in your industry and the greater economy? If the business you own is no longer right for you, is it time to consider meeting with a business broker to discuss selling your business and perhaps buying another business that is right for you?

If the business you own is right for you, it's time to decide whether you want to become a lifestyle business owner. If so, how would you like your business to be different from the way it is now? What does success look like to you? Write it out in as much detail as you can. Lifestyle business owners are not interested in how society defines success. What does success mean to you? Once you have a clear vision of what success looks like to you, it's time to set some goals. Perhaps you need to improve your profits so you can afford to hire a manager. Perhaps you need to overcome your fears of stepping back and letting the business run without your daily presence. Perhaps you'd like to accelerate the process of becoming a lifestyle business owner by attending one of our workshops or taking one of our online courses. Everyone's journey is a little different. What is the next step for you right now? As I look back on my journey, I am often surprised by how far I've come and how fortunate I've been. I grew up in a small town, and my parents were divorced when I was young. My parents were not wealthy, and I was just an average kid. School was hard for me, and I never went to college. I had a dream to succeed, and I was willing to work hard. Some of the businesses I got into failed miserably, but I never gave up. One step led to the next, and before I knew it, I was the lifestyle business owner of eight companies.

You can do this. If you want to own a business that runs without you for the most part and gives you the income, free time, and contribution you desire, I invite you to join the movement of lifestyle business ownership. In a time when the economy is shaky and the world is full of uncertainties and changes, it is the lifestyle business owners who shine. A wise person once said, "It's not the insult that determines your fate but your reaction to it."

This is your time. Go out there and make things happen. It has been a privilege to be your guide. I can't wait to hear where your journey takes you, and I look forward to supporting you along the way.

—Aaron

TAKE YOUR BUSINESS TO THE NEXT LEVEL

FREE Bonus Videos

Visit www.LifestyleBusinessOwner.com to claim your free, bonus training videos that accompany this book. Discover powerful strategies and secrets to help you become a lifestyle business owner.

Lifestyle Business Owner Academy

An interactive, multiweek, online course that guides you through how to become a lifestyle business owner from start to finish. It is the most comprehensive course that will teach you step-by-step the strategies and tactics to buy a business, increase its profits, and make it run without you. Learn from the comfort of your own home on your own schedule. Learn more at www.LBOAcademy.com.

Business Acceleration Intensive

A life-changing, multiday seminar in which you get to meet and learn from Aaron and his team of advisors. This is an incredible networking and business acceleration opportunity. You will walk away with the knowledge, confidence, and contacts you need to take your business to the next level. Seating is limited. Join Aaron's e-mail list at www.LBOAcademy.com to be notified of when registration opens for the next Business Acceleration Intensive.

The Inner Circle

Once a year, a select group of people are invited to train with Aaron Muller in a private mastermind group. The mastermind is reserved for the most serious students only. The selection process is rigorous, and application is by invitation only.

ABOUT THE AUTHOR

Aaron Muller is the founder of Lifestyle Business Owner Academy and a serial entrepreneur who currently owns eight multimillion-dollar companies that run without him. He is a #1 international bestselling author and the world's leading trainer on owning a small business that runs without the owner.

Having never gone to college, Aaron learned everything in the school of hard knocks. After owning or co-owning more than twenty companies in the Pacific Northwest, Aaron has probably dealt with every problem a small business owner can face—from employee headaches, lack of profits, and lack of time to lack of enjoyment and lack of contribution. He founded Lifestyle Business Owner Academy and wrote *The Lifestyle Business Owner* to teach emerging entrepreneurs how to own a small business that generates a six-figure income, runs without the owner, and creates social good through the operations of the business.

Over the last fifteen years, Aaron has mentored thousands of small business owners as a business broker, consultant, and coach. Through his seminars, videos, and online courses, Aaron inspires a new wave of entrepreneurs to become lifestyle business owners.

Meet Aaron and receive free training at **www.LBOAcademy.com**

Morgan James
Speakers Group

We connect Morgan James published authors with live and online events and audiences who will benefit from their expertise.

Morgan James makes all of our titles available
through the Library for All Charity Organization.

www.LibraryForAll.org

Printed in the USA
CPSIA information can be obtained
at www.ICGtesting.com
JSHW022320140824
68134JS00019B/1202